KitchenAid 13-Cup *Exact Slice Food* Processor (w/ Dicing Kit K42600

"Another winning cookbook from ATK. . . . The folks at America's Test Kitchen apply their rigorous experiments to determine the facts about these pans."
BOOKLIST ON *COOK IT IN CAST IRON*

Selected as one of Amazon's Best Books of 2015 in the Cookbooks and Food Writing Category
AMAZON ON *THE COMPLETE VEGETARIAN COOKBOOK*

"An exceptional resource for novice canners, though preserving veterans will find plenty here to love as well."
LIBRARY JOURNAL (STARRED REVIEW) ON *FOOLPROOF PRESERVING*

"A terrifically accessible and useful guide to grilling in all its forms that sets a new bar for its competitors."
PUBLISHERS WEEKLY (STARRED REVIEW) ON *MASTER OF THE GRILL*

"The 21st-century *Fannie Farmer Cookbook* or *The Joy of Cooking*. If you had to have one cookbook and that's all you could have, this one would do it."
CBS SAN FRANCISCO ON *THE NEW FAMILY COOKBOOK*

"The sum total of exhaustive experimentation . . . anyone interested in gluten-free cookery simply shouldn't be without it."
NIGELLA LAWSON ON *THE HOW CAN IT BE GLUTEN-FREE COOKBOOK*

"This book upgrades slow cooking for discriminating, 21st-century palates—that is indeed revolutionary."
THE DALLAS MORNING NEWS ON *SLOW COOKER REVOLUTION*

"The go-to gift book for newlyweds, small families, or empty nesters."
ORLANDO SENTINEL ON *THE COMPLETE COOKING FOR TWO COOKBOOK*

"Some 2,500 photos walk readers through 600 painstakingly tested recipes, leaving little room for error."
ASSOCIATED PRESS ON *THE AMERICA'S TEST KITCHEN COOKING SCHOOL COOKBOOK*

"A one-volume kitchen seminar, addressing in one smart chapter after another the sometimes surprising whys behind a cook's best practices. . . . You get the myth, the theory, the science, and the proof, all rigorously interrogated as only America's Test Kitchen can do."
NPR ON *THE SCIENCE OF GOOD COOKING*

"The perfect kitchen home companion. . . . The practical side of things is very much on display . . . cook-friendly and kitchen-oriented, illuminating the process of preparing food instead of mystifying it."
THE WALL STREET JOURNAL ON *THE COOK'S ILLUSTRATED COOKBOOK*

"This encyclopedia of meat cookery would feel completely overwhelming if it weren't so meticulously organized and artfully designed. This is *Cook's Illustrated* at its finest."
THE KITCHN ON *THE COOK'S ILLUSTRATED MEAT BOOK*

"This book is a comprehensive, no-nonsense guide . . . a well-thought-out, clearly explained primer for every aspect of home baking."
THE WALL STREET JOURNAL ON *THE COOK'S ILLUSTRATED BAKING BOOK*

"There are pasta books . . . and then there's this pasta book. Flip your carbohydrate dreams upside down and strain them through this sieve of revolutionary, creative, and also traditional recipes."
SAN FRANCISCO BOOK REVIEW ON *PASTA REVOLUTION*

"Further proof that practice makes perfect, if not transcendent. . . . If an intermediate cook follows the directions exactly, the results will be better than takeout or Mom's."
THE NEW YORK TIMES ON *THE NEW BEST RECIPE*

FOOD PROCESSOR

PERFECTION

75 Amazing Ways to Use the
Most Powerful Tool in Your Kitchen

the Editors at America's Test Kitchen

Library of Congress Cataloging-in-Publication Data

Names: America's Test Kitchen (Firm)
Title: Food processor perfection : 75 amazing ways to use the most powerful tool in your kitchen / by the editors at America's Test Kitchen.
Other titles: America's test kitchen (Television program)
Description: Brookline, MA : America's Test Kitchen, [2017] | Includes index.
Identifiers: LCCN 2016051195 | ISBN 9781940352909
Subjects: LCSH: Food processor cooking. | LCGFT: Cookbooks.
Classification: LCC TX840.F6 F68 2017 | DDC 641.5 /892--dc23
LC record available at https://lccn.loc.gov/2016051195

AMERICA'S TEST KITCHEN
17 Station Street, Brookline, MA 02445
Manufactured in Canada

10 9 8 7 6 5 4 3 2 1

Distributed by Penguin Random House Publisher Services
Tel: 800.733.3000

CHIEF CREATIVE OFFICER Jack Bishop
EDITORIAL DIRECTOR, BOOKS Elizabeth Carduff
EXECUTIVE EDITOR Julia Collin Davison
EXECUTIVE EDITOR Adam Kowit
EXECUTIVE FOOD EDITOR Dan Zuccarello
SENIOR EDITOR Sara Mayer
ASSOCIATE EDITORS Rachel Greenhaus, Lawman Johnson, and Russell Selander
TEST COOK Kathryn Callahan
EDITORIAL ASSISTANT Alyssa Langer
ART DIRECTOR Carole Goodman
ASSOCIATE ART DIRECTORS Allison Boales and Jen Kanavos Hoffman
PRODUCTION DESIGNER Reinaldo Cruz
DESIGNER Katie Barranger
PHOTOGRAPHY DIRECTOR Julie Bozzo Cote
ASSISTANT PHOTOGRAPHY PRODUCER Mary Ball
SENIOR STAFF PHOTOGRAPHER Daniel J. van Ackere
STAFF PHOTOGRAPHER Steve Klise
PHOTOGRAPHY Keller + Keller and Carl Tremblay
FOOD STYLING Isabelle English, Catrine Kelty, Marie Piraino, Maeve Sheridan, and Sally Staub
PHOTOSHOOT KITCHEN TEAM
  SENIOR EDITOR Chris O'Connor
  ASSOCIATE EDITOR Daniel Cellucci
  TEST COOK Matthew Fairman
  ASSISTANT TEST COOK Mady Nichas
ILLUSTRATION Jay Layman
PRODUCTION DIRECTOR Guy Rochford
SENIOR PRODUCTION MANAGER Jessica Lindheimer Quirk
PRODUCTION MANAGER Christine Walsh
IMAGING MANAGER Lauren Robbins
PRODUCTION AND IMAGING SPECIALISTS Heather Dube, Sean MacDonald, Dennis Noble, and Jessica Voas
COPY EDITOR Barbara Wood
PROOFREADER Amanda Poulsen Dix
INDEXER Elizabeth Parson

CONTENTS

WELCOME TO AMERICA'S TEST KITCHEN

This book has been tested, written, and edited by the folks at America's Test Kitchen, a very real 2,500-square-foot kitchen located just outside of Boston. It is the home of *Cook's Illustrated* magazine and *Cook's Country* magazine and is the Monday-through-Friday destination for more than 60 test cooks, editors, and cookware specialists. Our mission is to test recipes over and over again until we understand how and why they work and until we arrive at the "best" version.

We start the process of testing a recipe with a complete lack of preconceptions, which means that we accept no claim, no technique, and no recipe at face value. We simply assemble as many variations as possible, test a half-dozen of the most promising, and taste the results blind. We then construct our own recipe and continue to test it, varying ingredients, techniques, and cooking times until we reach a consensus. As we like to say in the test kitchen, "We make the mistakes so you don't have to." The result, we hope, is the best version of a particular recipe, but we realize that only you can be the final judge of our success (or failure). We use the same rigorous approach when we test equipment and taste ingredients.

All of this would not be possible without a belief that good cooking, much like good music, is based on a foundation of objective technique. Some people like spicy foods and others don't, but there is a right way to sauté, there is a best way to cook a pot roast, and there are measurable scientific principles involved in producing perfectly beaten, stable egg whites. Our ultimate goal is to investigate the fundamental principles of cooking to give you the techniques, tools, and ingredients you need to become a better cook. It is as simple as that.

To see what goes on behind the scenes at America's Test Kitchen, check out our social media channels for kitchen snapshots, exclusive content, video tips, and much more. You can watch us work (in our actual test kitchen) by tuning in to *America's Test Kitchen* or *Cook's Country from America's Test Kitchen* on public television or on our websites. Listen to test kitchen experts on public radio (SplendidTable.org) to hear insights that illuminate the truth about real home cooking. Want to hone your cooking skills or finally learn how to bake—with an America's Test Kitchen test cook? Enroll in one of our online cooking classes. If the big questions about the hows and whys of food science are your passion, join our Cook's Science experts for a deep dive. However you choose to visit us, we welcome you into our kitchen, where you can stand by our side as we test our way to the best recipes in America.

facebook.com/AmericasTestKitchen
twitter.com/TestKitchen
youtube.com/AmericasTestKitchen
instagram.com/TestKitchen
pinterest.com/TestKitchen
google.com/+AmericasTestKitchen

AmericasTestKitchen.com
CooksIllustrated.com
CooksCountry.com
CooksScience.com
OnlineCookingSchool.com

INTRODUCTION

The first food processors were giant, expensive, heavy-duty models invented to help make prep easier for restaurant chefs working on an enormous scale, but starting in the 1970s, smaller, more affordable versions of this invaluable tool appeared that were adapted for the home kitchen. Self-described "gadget freak" Julia Child called the food processor "one of the greatest breakthroughs since the mixer"; she was especially excited that it would allow home cooks "to make fish mousse in a few seconds." The food processor quickly changed the way cooks thought about preparing ingredients and making complex recipes, and it helped eliminate the need for piles of other, more specialized equipment, making all kinds of dishes more accessible.

These days, the food processor is a fixture in most well-equipped kitchens, yet we think it's often underutilized and underappreciated. Too many cooks see their food processor as a bulky, specialized item worth dragging out for only a few specific tasks. We want to show just how diverse its applications can be, for cooking as well as for baking.

In the test kitchen, the food processor is an everyday tool. We love all the ways it makes ingredient prep faster and helps us get better results in everything from dips to bread doughs. We've also spent years discovering which unexpected tasks can be made easier with an assist from this powerhouse appliance. These include grinding meat for fantastic homemade burgers of all kinds, creating simple batters, and making sophisticated frozen desserts that would typically require a fancy ice cream maker. In creating this book, we wanted to explore the range of dishes that can be streamlined and simplified when you use a food processor, plus share all our tips and tricks for making the most of this kitchen workhorse. We organized the book to emphasize the machine's varied abilities and multifaceted uses. For instance, in our Sliced Green Salad (page 36), not only did we whiz together a perfect vinaigrette, we also sliced all the vegetables, including the lettuce. The custom-ground mixture of short ribs and steak tips in our Meatballs and Marinara (page 96) gave us meltingly tender meatballs, and the processor made it easy to throw together a rich homemade sauce to simmer them in. And notoriously fussy Classic Cheesecake (page 158) was a cinch when we whipped up the silky-smooth filling and quick crust in the processor.

While this book may not feature a fish mousse recipe, it does have everything from Homemade Italian-Style Sausages and Peppers (page 94) to Free-Form Summer Fruit Tart (page 142)—so we think Julia would approve. It also contains our exhaustively researched buying guide, with detailed reviews of processors, large and small, plus all the tricks we've learned, like using vegetable oil spray to keep sticky ingredients from gumming up the shredding disk or grinding your own nut flours in the processor. Whether you're new to using a food processor and looking for a comprehensive guide to this hardworking kitchen tool or you're in search of ways to make better use of a processor you've had in your cupboard for years, this book will show you how to make it your new sous-chef and an indispensable part of your day-to-day life in the kitchen, no matter what you're cooking.

FOOD PROCESSOR 101

ANATOMY OF A GREAT FOOD PROCESSOR

After more than 20 years of working with food processors in the test kitchen, we've come up with a checklist that determines how well any individual model will handle core tasks from slicing tomatoes to kneading heavy pizza dough. Here are the elements that we've found to be the most important in a truly hardworking, all-star food processor.

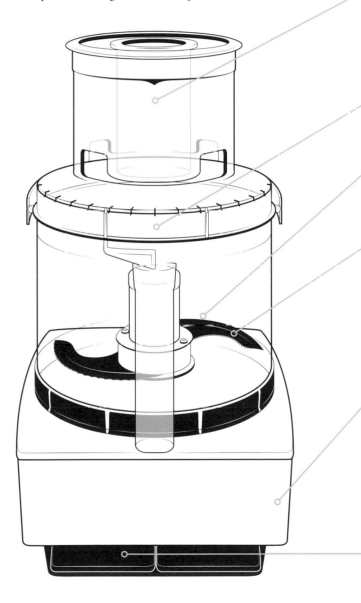

well-designed feed tube

The feed tube should be large enough to minimize the need for pretrimming ingredients and the possibility of food waste but also narrow enough to hold food upright. The amount you have to trim from ingredients will depend on the exact dimensions of the feed tube on your processor.

small space between disks and feed tube

This element of food processor design ensures that all the food gets shredded or sliced instead of getting stuck between the disk and the bottom of the feed tube. The disks should also be easy to change and should securely attach to the processor.

minimal gaps between blade and bowl

The space between the end of the blade and the side of the bowl as well as the space between the base of the blade and the bottom of the bowl should be small—3 to 4 millimeters is ideal. This ensures thorough mixing and even chopping. If the space is too large, food can get stuck under the blade or along the sides of the bowl and won't get processed.

sharp, efficient metal blade

A food processor blade can't be sharpened at home the way a knife can, so it has to be great right out of the box. We use the metal chopping blade more than any other blade or disk on our food processor—even for mixing and kneading doughs, since the stubby plastic "dough blade" tends to leave unmixed pockets of flour and takes longer to bring dough together. A sharp blade that safely and easily attaches to the processor is key.

weighty, compact base

The right base helps give your food processor a smaller, space-saving footprint on the counter and keeps the machine anchored during heavy mixing.

responsive pulse button

Recipes often call for "one-second pulses," but not all machines do the same thing when you use the pulse function. Some blades continue to rotate for a second after you lift your finger off the button. Others have a quick stop-start that we prefer; ingredients are instantly tossed around the bowl and into the cutting action. Test your processor to see exactly what happens when you push the pulse button, and use that to inform the way you use this function.

THE TEST KITCHEN'S GUIDE TO BUYING A FOOD PROCESSOR

In the test kitchen, we demand a food processor that can handle lots of chopping, slicing, and shredding while delivering professional-quality results, and we think home cooks deserve the same. It had better be able not only to puree a dip and whip up creamy mayonnaise but also to cut fat into a pie dough in seconds, grind beef into hamburger, and knead heavy pizza dough. And of course we want our food processor to be simple to use and quick to clean. We bought eight full-size food processors, priced from $59.99 to $299.99, with capacities of 11 to 14 cups, a size we deemed big enough to handle most recipes. We put each model through 21 tests, measuring their performance on a range of tasks and comparing construction and user-friendliness. We considered everything from the feel of the pulse button and the shape of the workbowl to the capacity of the feed tube and how often we'd have to handle sharp blades. In terms of blades, some models were equipped with just the basics—a chopping blade and a shredding/slicing disk—and others arrived with boxes of extra attachments. We assessed which of these were actually useful and which were just window dressing.

On the Chopping Block

While food processors are designed for a variety of jobs, we most often use them for chopping, so we ran several chopping tests and weighted those results heaviest in our final ratings: prepping *mirepoix* (a combination of diced carrot, celery, and onion used as a foundation for many sauces, soups, and stews), grinding almonds, mincing parsley, and grinding chunks of beef. We wanted to achieve uniform pieces of food at whatever size we desired. One of the biggest factors in chopping performance was the length of time the machine ran once we'd pushed the pulse button—short, powerful, jerky pulsing is essential to toss ingredients around the bowl and into the cutting action. The other important factor was the distance between the blade and the bottom and sides of the workbowl. Smaller gaps were critical to making sure that chunks of food didn't escape the blade.

Any Way You Slice It

Slicing and shredding with a food processor can be a huge timesaver. A good machine takes just seconds to produce piles of carrot shreds, mounds of shredded cheese, or pounds of potato slices. We shredded soft cheddar cheese and crunchy carrots, and we sliced delicate tomatoes and firm potatoes,

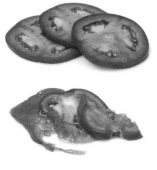
considering not just the quality of the processed food but also how much was wasted, whether trapped in the machine or pretrimmed so the food would fit inside feed tubes. Blade quality mattered, too: Dull blades bruised and hacked up the food, splattering the workbowl with juices. The top machines had sharp, efficient blades that made clean, dry cuts.

Mixing It Up

Efficient mixing is a key feature. We tried making pie crust, kneading dough, and mixing mayonnaise on each machine, and also assessed the mixing action by processing yogurt with drops of yellow and blue food coloring, timing how long it took to turn green. Better models created an even green hue in 25 seconds or less. Mayonnaise was a failure point for several machines. Once again, most of the failures seemed to be caused by excessive space between the blade and the bottom of the bowl.

When it came to pushing the machines' upper limits, double batches of pizza dough were a real challenge for a few models. The KitchenAid model shut itself down repeatedly. A light flashed on the Breville, indicating distress, and the Cuisinart Elemental model left clumps of flour. The manual of the Hamilton Beach said it was not meant for dough; when we gave it a try anyway, it made a lot of noise and jumped around the counter, but the dough actually emerged in good shape. (We don't recommend processing dough in this model routinely since it could burn out the motor over time.) The top performers, including our front-runner, yielded silky, bouncy dough with little apparent strain.

Next, we pureed 28-ounce cans of whole tomatoes. While most models handled this task acceptably well, it made us wonder how much liquid the workbowls could hold without leaking. We filled each with water to its maximum volume and ran them on high. A few erupted in overflowing waves, and a few more sent forth a steady trickle. Our favorite never spilled a drop.

Wash 'n' Go

Cleanup was the final factor. Nooks and crannies inside the lid and on the pusher and feed tubes of the KitchenAid 11-cup model trapped food and were a chore to clean and dry. The same applied to multipart shafts that held blades inside workbowls on other models. Our favorite machines had smooth, simple surfaces that were a snap to clean and dry. Our favorite models' workbowls are all dishwasher-safe (blades should be hand washed to keep them sharp).

In the end, nothing beat the **Cuisinart Custom 14 Food Processor**. It is not the cheapest model available, but it proves its worth in its sturdiness and performance, and it outshone several more expensive models. It comes with just three basic blades, for chopping, slicing, and shredding. After all of our testing, we found that these are all you really need for most jobs (though Cuisinart offers additional blades on its website). With a plain, heavy base; two simple, lever-style bars to operate; a responsive pulsing action; a sharp blade set close to the base and bottom of the workbowl; and a pared-down design that is easy to clean, handle, and store, this machine has everything we want in a food processor.

Cuisinart
Custom 14 Food Processor

MODEL DFP-14BCNY
PRICE $199.99
MINI BOWL None
LEAKING? No

CHOPPING ★★★
SLICING ★★★
SHREDDING ★★★
MIXING ★★★
PUREEING ★★★
EASE OF USE ★★★

With a powerful, quiet motor; responsive pulsing action; sharp blades; and a simple design, our winner aced every test, surprising us time and again by outshining pricier competitors. It was one of the few models that didn't leak at its maximum stated liquid capacity. It's also easy to clean and store. Additional blade options are available à la carte. See the note on page 3 for information about Cuisinart's recent redesign of its chopping blade and recall of blades on older models.

The Breville
Sous Chef 12-Cup Food Processor

MODEL BFP660SIL
PRICE $299.99
MINI BOWL None
LEAKING? No

CHOPPING ★★★
SLICING ★★★
SHREDDING ★★★
MIXING ★★
PUREEING ★★★
EASE OF USE ★★½

Quiet and quick at most tasks, with a well-designed workbowl that slides smoothly into place and pours neatly, this model excelled at chopping, slicing, and shredding, but its motor clearly struggled when mixing a double batch of pizza dough. And with blades spinning out of reach in the big bowl, mayonnaise never emulsified and dyed yogurt never turned uniformly green. Turning the shaft on the slicing blade offered eight thickness settings clearly marked in millimeters, a nice design touch.

Black + Decker
Performance Food Processor

MODEL FP6010B
PRICE $149.99
MINI BOWL 4 cups
LEAKING? No

CHOPPING ★★½
SLICING ★★★
SHREDDING ★★★
MIXING ★★★
PUREEING ★★
EASE OF USE ★½

This model performed surprisingly well in many areas, despite a cheap feel to its construction. The tall, skinny accessory box shattered after taking a tumble. Suction-cup feet on its lightweight base failed to stabilize the machine when it was working, and its motor was loud. The pulse button continued running a bit long, and chopping was a bit uneven. That said, its slicing and shredding were impressive, and its dicing attachment worked very well.

Cuisinart
Elite Collection 2.0 12-Cup Food Processor

MODEL FP-12DC
PRICE $249.00
MINI BOWL 4 cups
LEAKING? Yes

CHOPPING ★★½
SLICING ★★
SHREDDING ★★★
MIXING ★★
PUREEING ★★½
EASE OF USE ★★½

We liked this machine's responsive pulse button and simple controls; shredding was exemplary, and chopping was more than acceptable. But the motor struggled when mixing heavy pizza dough, and flour flew up into the lid and fell out messily after making pie crust. Nooks and crannies in the workbowl lid slowed cleanup. See the note on page 3 for information about Cuisinart's recent redesign of its chopping blade and recall of blades on older models.

recommended with reservations (continued)   performance   comments

Cuisinart
Elemental 11 Food Processor

MODEL FP-11GM
PRICE $149.00
MINI BOWL None
LEAKING? No

CHOPPING ★★½
SLICING ★★★
SHREDDING ★★
MIXING ★★½
PUREEING ★★½
EASE OF USE ★½

With a lid that usually went on a bit stiffly and off-kilter, this machine took some work to open and close, and its lightweight base and parts felt less solidly constructed than its Cuisinart siblings. The motor was very loud. Too-long, too-weak pulses made the chopping action less efficient, as did a narrower blade that left gaps around the edges for food to slip through. Pizza dough was a struggle. See the note on page 3 for information about Cuisinart's recent redesign of its chopping blade and recall of blades on older models.

not recommended

Hamilton Beach
Stack & Snap Food Processor

MODEL 70725
PRICE $59.99
MINI BOWL None
LEAKING? Yes

CHOPPING ★★
SLICING ★★★
SHREDDING ★½
MIXING ★½
PUREEING ★★
EASE OF USE ★★

This model's claim to fame is that the workbowl and lid snap on with no twisting, but the plastic flaps that hold down the lid felt like they might break off. More critically, gaps between blade and bowl allowed food to sit on the bottom and avoid the chopping overhead. It failed to make mayonnaise, and it leaked when filled with liquid to capacity. Lightweight, inexpensive construction meant the machine wobbled on its suction-cup feet. Though we made pizza dough in this model, the manual instructs not to use it for dough.

Oster
Designed for Life 14-Cup Food Processor with 5-Cup Mini Chopper

MODEL FPSTFP5273- DFL
PRICE $69.00
MINI BOWL 5 cups
LEAKING? No

CHOPPING ★★
SLICING ★
SHREDDING ★★½
MIXING ★★
PUREEING ★★½
EASE OF USE ★½

While this is one of the lowest-priced products in the lineup, it also felt lightweight and flimsy, and running it required earplugs (think jackhammer crossed with dentist drill: Ree! REE!). It wobbled on its suction-cup feet, pumped a stream of air at us as it ran, and blew flour and bits of food all over the interior of the workbowl like confetti. Gaps between blade and bowl allowed some pieces to pass under the blade unchopped, and mayonnaise failed to emulsify.

KitchenAid
11-Cup Food Processor with ExactSlice System

MODEL KFP1133
PRICE $199.95
MINI BOWL 3 cups
LEAKING? Yes

CHOPPING ★★
SLICING ★★★
SHREDDING ★½
MIXING ★★½
PUREEING ★★
EASE OF USE ½

With a remarkably stiff pulse button that was painful to push and somewhat unresponsive, comparatively weak chopping action, a draggy gasket that made the lid difficult to twist on and off, and abundant crannies that trapped food and moisture and made cleaning complicated, this machine made us work too hard. While its slicing was crisp and neat, the thickness-adjusting lever on the front is unmarked, so choosing a specific thickness involves trial, error, and wasted food.

SIZE DOES MATTER

The Sizes We Used for This Book

Every recipe in this book was successfully tested in our winning 14-cup processor. When we tested food processors, we focused on models that held 11 to 14 cups (see pages 4–5 for the full testing). These larger processors are fairly common, and successful models can handle both large and very small amounts of ingredients. However, we know that food processors come in many other sizes, so we also tested the recipes in this book in a variety of other models, and each recipe includes a note about which sizes can be used to prepare it. Many can be made in machines as small as 7 cups with no issues. A few can even be prepared successfully in the mini processors that are increasingly common on the market (we tested them in our winning 4-cup mini processor). Make sure you know the size of your food processor before attempting a recipe—if you overload the bowl, you risk damaging the motor on your processor, ruining your recipe, and making a big mess.

Small Food Processors

While we consider our winning 14-cup food processor indispensable, standard food processors tend to be big and pricey. Smaller processors are a good choice for budget- or space-conscious cooks or for those who want to dip a toe in the processor pond before shelling out nearly $200. We took a look at the small food processors on the market to find the most versatile, efficient, and well-designed model. We zeroed in on 3- to 6-cup models, of which we found seven, priced from $27.99 to $99.99. We put the processors through their paces: mincing garlic; dicing celery, onions, and carrots; grating Parmesan cheese; chopping almonds; and making mayonnaise, pesto, and hummus.

Size was an important factor: 3.5- and 4-cup models were ideal. They were compact yet large enough to handle a range of projects. Powerful-yet-responsive controls were optimal. Feed tubes are essential for making mayonnaise in a food processor: The oil has to be added slowly to properly emulsify with the other ingredients. The final key element is the blade—just as in our testing of full-size models, we liked sharp blades with low clearance between the blade and the bottom of the bowl. Blades with just 3 to 4 millimeters of clearance make better, more evenly processed food; any higher and food can get stranded underneath the blade and remain unprocessed.

There are downsides to smaller processors. First, they can't handle doughs well; their workbowls are too small and their motors too weak. Second, they're not efficient for large-quantity prep—they don't have grating or slicing blades, and their smaller workbowls maxed out at about 2 cups of vegetables. But a good small food processor can excel at mayonnaises, dressings, dips, marinades, and sauces—projects

ATTACHMENTS DISORDER

Most full-size food processors come with a couple of standard attachments, and you can usually buy a variety of other additions to augment the capabilities of your processor. Extra slicing disks and blades made for cutting more finely or in specific shapes (like French fries or a julienne) might be useful depending on how you want to use your processor. However, while some of the available attachments are surprisingly well designed, many are completely useless.

We like processors that offer a mini bowl, which is simply a smaller processor bowl that fits on the full-size processor base. The mini bowl basically turns your full-size processor into a mini processor, making it perfect for small-batch tasks and allowing you to handle two separate jobs without any dishwashing in between. In the past, we also liked attachments that let your food processor function as a citrus juicer. However, we rejected contraptions like a dough hook attachment (the metal blade does just fine) and a "continuous feed chute" that purported to turn the processor into a Salad Shooter–type device.

that would otherwise require serious muscle or a food mill. They can also handle smaller-quantity mincing, grinding, and dicing. You need a full-size processor for most of the recipes in this book, but if you're looking for a tool to make prep easier in the kitchen, the **Cuisinart Elite Collection 4-Cup Chopper/Grinder** ($59.95)—at half the size and less than a third of the price of our winning full-size machine—is the best small food processor on the market.

Oversized, Overpriced, Underperforming

Alongside our full-size and mini food processor testings, we also tried two high-end, extra-large food processors, the 16-Cup KitchenAid ProLine Series ($699.95) and the Waring Commercial 3.5-Quart Pro Food Processor ($426.93), running them through the same tests as the average-priced models to see whether their "professional" designation made any difference in their performance, and whether they offered any extra features that made them worth nearly two to three times the price of an ordinary food processor.

WHAT SIZE DO I NEED?

The majority of the recipes in this book—almost 80%—can be successfully prepared in a 7-cup food processor. But some recipes require a larger processor, either because of the sheer volume of ingredients being used, as with the batter for our Carrot Layer Cake (page 138), or the type of processing being done, such as whipping cream. And you'll need an 11- or 14-cup food processor if you're planning to knead dough, depending on the recipe. For specifics, see the list below; any recipe in the book that is not listed here will work in a 7-cup or larger processor.

Our conclusion? The Waring is nice, a souped-up version of our winning model, the Cuisinart Custom 14, made by its sister company. However, its performance in a few key areas, including chopping and slicing, actually fell short of our winner. The KitchenAid ProLine is a space-hogging behemoth at more than 16 pounds, 18 inches high, and 12 inches wide, and it includes an equally enormous accessories box. Like the Waring, its performance also fell short of the top average-priced models. While the performance of both models was not bad, we can't recommend spending this much for less-than-stellar results. We'll be sticking with the practical, affordable workhorse that is our winner.

The recipes in this book use the food processor to tackle an enormous range of ingredients—fruits, vegetables, meat, fish, legumes, grains, nuts—and techniques, including slicing, shredding, chopping, grinding, and pureeing. You should always consult your food processor manual for specific instructions on how to use each function, but in this section we also provide an overview of a few of the key techniques we use in this book and some of our discoveries for making the most of your processor in each capacity.

1 using the slicing disk

Our winning processor comes with a standard 4mm slicing disk, which is what we used for all the recipes in this book. Some food processors have adjustable blades so you can change the thickness of the slices; you can also purchase smaller or larger slicing disks for most models. The way you feed ingredients into the processor affects the slices, so pay attention to the orientation of the ingredient in the feed tube. For instance, for meat like skirt steak, we make sure to feed the meat in so it gets sliced against the grain to ensure tender results. Slicing works best with firm ingredients, so we partially freeze the meat before slicing it and prefer tightly packed greens, like the heart of romaine in photo 1. (You can also roll greens like kale to create a tightly packed bundle for slicing.)

2 using the feed tube

Choose the right feed tube—small or large—for your ingredients so that you can pack them tightly; you'll get cleaner, more consistent results if they don't have room to move around. Whole potatoes, onions, and big pieces like wedges of cabbage benefit from the larger tube, while smaller amounts of narrower carrots, zucchini, and celery work best in the smaller one. Depending on the size of your ingredient, you may need to do some trimming before placing it in the feed tube. Use steady pressure when pushing food through the tube into the

blades. If you're slicing several different ingredients that will ultimately be combined, you can even put them all into the feed tube together, as with the salad vegetables in photos 2a and 2b.

3 adding liquid to a running processor

We frequently call for adding liquid ingredients to the processor in a slow, steady stream while it's running. This not only helps ensure that the liquid ingredients get mixed evenly into the rest of the ingredients, but it can also help create a smooth emulsion in recipes, like the mayonnaise shown in photo 3, where you are mixing together two liquids that don't normally combine.

4 chopping, mincing, and grinding

Our best advice for chopping in the processor is to err on the side of under-processing; you can always give the ingredients another pulse to chop them more finely, but you can't go back. For this precise reason, we tend to use the pulse function instead of the processing function when chopping, grinding, or mincing ingredients in the food processor. Pulsing food offers more control than processing it; the food is chopped more evenly because the ingredients are redistributed—akin to stirring—with every pulse. This allows you more control over the final texture, as with the Cauliflower Rice (page 45) in photos 4a and 4b.

5 using the shredding disk

The shredding disk can shred all kind of ingredients into small, even pieces. You can power through pounds of cheese, potatoes, and more in just seconds. Unlike with slicing, it doesn't matter as much what shape or size the ingredients are when they go into the processor for shredding, but similar to slicing, it's easier to shred firm ingredients like the carrots shown in photo 5, so we recommend chilling foods such as semisoft cheese before shredding. To make cleanup easier, spray the feed tube, disk, and workbowl with a light coating of vegetable oil spray before you begin to keep the ingredients from gumming up the shredding disk.

6 mixing and pureeing

As ingredients are mixed or pureed in the food processor, the mixture often clings to the sides of the workbowl and thus some parts of it may not get fully processed. This is why it's crucial to scrape down the workbowl at various stages in recipes that use those functions of the food processor, as shown in photo 6. We recommend using a silicone spatula for this process; be careful not to cut the spatula on the processor blade.

7 batters and doughs

Using the food processor to mix up batters and doughs is definitely faster than mixing by hand, and it's also more efficient than using a stand mixer. However, overprocessing can lead to mediocre results, so follow the processing times in the recipes and pay attention to the order in which the ingredients are added. We tend to add flour last to ensure the gluten won't get overdeveloped and lead to tough cookies or cakes. In bread doughs, where gluten development is a good thing, be sure to follow visual cues to make sure the dough is fully kneaded, as shown in photo 7.

Process with Less Mess

Food processors are real timesavers while you're cooking, but cleaning them can be quite annoying—and time-consuming. We've developed our recipes to minimize the number of times you'll have to wipe out the processor or wash it completely clean during a particular recipe when you move from processing one ingredient to another, and we've also come up with a few quick tips for making cleanup easier when a recipe is finished.

keep your lid clean
If you're not using the feed tube, cover the workbowl with plastic wrap before processing, then fit the lid directly over the plastic. After processing, simply discard the splattered plastic and put the clean lid back on the shelf.

put a cork in it
To give a dirty processor bowl a good soak, put a wine or champagne cork in the center hole. Now you can fill the bowl all the way to the top with hot water.

clean in a whizz
To quickly rinse the workbowl between tasks, add a few drops of dish soap and warm water to the liquid fill line, run the machine for a few seconds, and rinse the bowl well.

THE POWER OF THE FOOD PROCESSOR: BY THE NUMBERS

To prove that a food processor really saves time, we ran a few comparative experiments. We think the results speak for themselves:

kneading bread dough	
In stand mixer	12 minutes
In food processor	2 minutes
kneading pizza dough	
By hand	8 minutes
In stand mixer	5 minutes
In food processor	2 minutes
whipping cream	
In stand mixer	3 minutes
In food processor	1 minute
making vinaigrette	
By hand	3 minutes
In food processor	2 minutes
making layer cake	
Without processor	4 bowls
With processor	1 bowl
shredding carrots	
By hand	¾ cup in 1 minute
With food processor	6 cups in 1 minute

WHEN NOT TO USE A FOOD PROCESSOR

The food processor is definitely our first choice for home cooks if they're only going to buy one small appliance, but it does have a few limitations. (We also highly recommend you invest in a stand mixer and a blender.) We've found that many food processors tend to leak when filled with liquid, although this isn't a problem with our winning model. Because of this, blenders are still our first choice for handling tasks that involve mostly liquid ingredients, including making smoothies and pureeing soups, since a blender is designed to funnel all the ingredients downward in the tapered jar toward the multipronged blade. Similarly, if we're beating a large amount of egg whites, we still prefer using a stand mixer with a whisk attachment because the ingredients have more space to expand.

EIGHT CLEVER USES FOR A FOOD PROCESSOR

1 crush ice
You probably never thought of your food processor as a bar tool, but it's a perfect way to create cocktail-worthy crushed ice. Simply pulse up to 2 cups ice cubes in the processor until finely ground, 8 to 10 pulses.

2 whip cream
Process 1½ cups heavy cream, 2 tablespoons sugar, and ½ teaspoon vanilla extract to soft peaks, about 1 minute, for a superquick basic sweetened whipped cream.

3 make bread crumbs
Making your own bread crumbs lets you control the size, and you can also use any kind of bread you want. Simply tear the bread into pieces and then pulse in the food processor until ground to the desired texture.

4 create flavored salts
Process ½ cup coarse sea salt with ½ cup fresh rosemary or thyme leaves until finely ground, about 30 seconds. Store in the refrigerator for 1 week.

5 grind nut flours
In this book we process nuts in several different ways—from simply chopped to a coarse meal to completely ground to a paste. The difference is simply how long you process the nuts. The more you process them, the more oil they release, taking them closer and closer to nut butter. For nut flour, pulse 2 cups whole almonds, cashews, hazelnuts, peanuts, or pistachios until finely ground, 16 to 20 pulses. You'll end up with about 2½ cups of flour.

6 make a brown sugar substitute
Most brown sugar is made by adding molasses either to granulated white sugar or to sugarcane syrup before it has crystallized. You can make a quick substitute by pulsing 1 cup granulated sugar with 1 tablespoon molasses for light brown sugar or 2 tablespoons molasses for dark brown sugar.

7 grind your own superfine sugar
Superfine sugar's small granules dissolve almost instantly, so it's ideal for sweetening drinks as well as for baked applications where you want a grit-free texture. To make your own, process 1 cup plus 2 teaspoons granulated sugar for 30 seconds. This yields about 1 cup of superfine sugar.

8 mix up flavored sugars
Flavored sugars are great in coffee or tea or sprinkled onto fruit or baked goods. Here are two of our favorites. For vanilla sugar, process ¼ fresh vanilla bean with 1 cup sugar for 45 seconds to 1 minute. For citrus sugar, add 2 teaspoons grated fresh lemon, lime, or orange zest to 1 cup sugar and pulse 20 times. Store in the refrigerator for up to 1 week.

PROCESS YOUR WAY TO PERFECT DIPS & SPREADS

With a food processor in regular rotation, homemade spreads and dips can be at the ready with hardly any fuss, livening up everything from a sandwich to a cocktail party spread to a pasta dinner. Plus, when your finger is on the pulse, so to speak, you control the consistency. Like your peanut butter a little chunkier or hummus a bit smoother? Up to you. You can also control exactly what goes into your mayonnaise, pesto, and salsa—skip the preservatives, sweeteners, and unnecessary additives for better-than-store-bought results. And mixing up the flavors of your favorite condiments and toppings has never been easier.

FOOD PROCESSOR FINDINGS

Here are a few tricks we've discovered for pureeing dips and spreads in your food processor:

1 Nuts have enough oil in them to make a great butter without any extra—all you have to do is wait. As you process, the blade will coax more and more oil out of the nuts until you end up with a creamy butter without the need to introduce any additional oil to the mix.

2 To adjust consistency and add textural interest to a mixture when you want most of it to be fully pureed, simply reserve a small amount of your ingredients to add later in the processing step—instant chunky peanut butter!

3 Since we can get a perfectly smooth and stable emulsification in the food processor, it's even easier to add extra flavorings for variations like our Homemade Smoked Paprika Mayonnaise (page 27)—the stable emulsion ensures that the spice is evenly blended throughout the mixture.

4 Sure, using a food processor helps you avoid fussy prep work, but we didn't realize the extent of what can be skipped. For our hummus, we didn't bother to remove all the slippery skins from the chickpeas, which conventional wisdom says have to be cleared off in order to get a really smooth, creamy hummus. Our technique gave us ideal results without this time-consuming step.

AMAZING EMULSIFICATION

An emulsion is a combination of liquids that wouldn't ordinarily mix, made by mixing them together so vigorously that one of the ingredients breaks down into tiny droplets—so tiny that they become suspended in the other liquid. Think about oil and vinegar after you shake them to make a vinaigrette. Unfortunately, as soon as you stop mixing, the dispersed droplets start to find each other and coalesce. Eventually, this causes the two liquids to separate again. The food processor helps make a much smoother and more stable emulsion, as do ingredients called emulsifiers, which help the liquids combine and stay that way by preventing the dispersed droplets from falling out of suspension. Egg yolks, mustard, and mayonnaise are common emulsifiers. The images below show a simple oil and vinegar vinaigrette (left) which separated after just 15 minutes, and a vinaigrette with added emulsifiers, which held a stable emulsion for 1½ hours.

just oil and vinegar   **oil, vinegar, mustard, and mayo**

QUICK TOMATO SALSA

makes about 3 cups   food processor size 7 to 14 cups

why this recipe works Compared with homemade salsa and its fresh flavor, jarred varieties are like faded photographs—ghosts of their former selves, often too wet and woefully underseasoned. It's not that we don't see the draw of the ready-made stuff: You open the jar, and you're done. But we were tired of having to choose between fast and flavor, so we set out to create a homemade salsa that would come together in almost as little time as it takes to open a jar, with minimal chopping. First, we reached for canned diced tomatoes. Convenient as they are, though, canned tomatoes come with a lot of juice, and juice makes for watery salsa. The fix was easy: Pour the tomatoes into a strainer and let the juice drain away. To make the salsa, we started with half a red onion, cilantro, jalapeños, garlic cloves, and lime juice in the processor bowl. To avoid the time-consuming tasks of seeding and removing the ribs of fresh chiles, we used jarred jalapeños. The food processor quickly and effortlessly chopped the ingredients to uniform size; after just a few pulses, everything came together. We held the tomatoes back until after the onion mixture had been pulsed so that they retained more texture. A final quick sit in the strainer removed all the extra moisture created during processing, and in the time that it took to drain, we opened a bag of tortilla chips to dig into this quick salsa. Because the method is so simple, our variations can add tons of flavor with almost no effort. You can substitute two fresh tomatoes, cored and cut into 1-inch pieces, for the canned tomatoes.

½ small red onion, cut into 1-inch pieces

½ cup fresh cilantro leaves

¼ cup jarred sliced jalapeños

2 tablespoons lime juice

2 garlic cloves, peeled and smashed

½ teaspoon salt

1 (28-ounce) can diced tomatoes, drained

Pulse onion, cilantro, jalapeños, lime juice, garlic, and salt in food processor until coarsely chopped, about 5 pulses. Add tomatoes and pulse until combined, about 3 pulses. Transfer salsa to fine-mesh strainer and let drain briefly; transfer to serving bowl. Serve. (Salsa can be refrigerated for up to 2 days.)

QUICK TOMATO AND BLACK BEAN SALSA
Add ½ teaspoon chili powder to food processor with onion. Stir 1 cup rinsed canned black beans into salsa before serving.

QUICK SMOKY TOMATO AND CORN SALSA
Substitute 1 (28-ounce) can fire-roasted diced tomatoes for diced tomatoes. Stir 1 cup thawed frozen corn into salsa before serving.

ARTICHOKE DIP

serves 6 to 8 **food processor size** 7 to 14 cups

why this recipe works For a version of this party favorite that's packed with flavor and super-scoopable, we turned to jarred artichokes, which have much better flavor than canned or frozen versions. Hearts labeled "baby" or "cocktail" proved to have the most tender meat and delicate leaves, with no textural flaws to detract from their bright, slightly acidic flavor. For the base of our dip, a simple mixture of cream cheese and Parmesan created the perfect creamy texture. The blend of cheeses added a nice tang without overwhelming the lemony, briny sweetness of the artichokes. We simply processed the cheeses with the artichoke hearts and some smashed garlic for a smooth, flavorful dip. Our variations mix up the flavors of this dip without sacrificing the simple technique and smooth texture. While we prefer the flavor and texture of jarred whole baby artichokes, you can substitute 9 ounces of frozen artichoke hearts, thawed and patted dry, for the jarred. To soften cream cheese quickly, microwave it for 20 to 30 seconds.

1½ cups jarred whole baby artichoke hearts packed in water, rinsed and patted dry

8 ounces cream cheese, softened

1 ounce Parmesan cheese, grated (½ cup)

2 garlic cloves, peeled and smashed

Salt and pepper

1 tablespoon minced fresh chives

Process artichokes, cream cheese, Parmesan, and garlic with ¼ teaspoon salt and ⅛ teaspoon pepper in food processor until mostly smooth, about 1 minute, scraping down sides of bowl as needed. Transfer dip to serving bowl, cover, and refrigerate until flavors meld, about 30 minutes. Season with salt and pepper to taste. Sprinkle with chives and serve. (Dip can be refrigerated for up to 1 day.)

ARTICHOKE AND FAVA BEAN DIP
Substitute ½ cup frozen fava beans, thawed, for ½ cup artichokes. Add ¼ cup fresh mint leaves to food processor with artichokes.

ARTICHOKE DIP WITH GOAT CHEESE AND THYME
Substitute 8 ounces softened goat cheese for cream cheese. Add 1 teaspoon fresh thyme leaves to food processor with artichokes.

HERBED SPINACH DIP

serves 4 to 6   food processor size 7 to 14 cups

why this recipe works If it's not properly prepared, spinach dip can end up a chunky, watery mess, with stringy pieces of spinach and almost no flavor. For a spinach dip to really taste good, we found that both the ingredients and the method were key. We enriched our dip with equal amounts of mayonnaise and sour cream. Herbs, red bell pepper, scallions, garlic, and even a little kick of hot sauce helped pack in tons of bright flavor (and great texture). Our variations incorporated even more substantial additions like bacon and feta cheese. For the mixing method, the food processor was the perfect tool to chop the thawed spinach to a very fine consistency and distribute it evenly throughout the dip along with all the other ingredients. Serve with crudités or chips.

10 ounces frozen chopped spinach, thawed and squeezed dry

½ red bell pepper, cut into 1-inch pieces

½ cup sour cream

½ cup mayonnaise

½ cup fresh parsley leaves

1 tablespoon fresh dill fronds or 1 teaspoon dried dill weed

3 scallions, cut into 1-inch lengths

1 garlic clove, peeled and smashed

¼ teaspoon hot sauce

Salt and pepper

Process all ingredients with ½ teaspoon salt and ¼ teaspoon pepper in food processor until mostly smooth, about 1 minute, scraping down sides of bowl as needed. Transfer dip to serving bowl, cover, and refrigerate until flavors meld, about 30 minutes. Season with salt and pepper to taste. Serve. (Dip can be refrigerated for up to 1 day.)

SPINACH DIP WITH BLUE CHEESE AND BACON

Omit bell pepper, dill, ½ teaspoon salt, and hot sauce. Add ⅓ cup crumbled blue cheese to food processor with spinach. Sprinkle dip with 2 slices cooked, crumbled bacon before serving.

SPINACH DIP WITH FETA, LEMON, AND OREGANO

Omit bell pepper, dill, and ½ teaspoon salt. Add ½ cup crumbled feta cheese, 2 tablespoons fresh oregano, 1 tablespoon lemon juice, and 1 teaspoon grated lemon zest to food processor with spinach.

CLASSIC HUMMUS

makes about 2 cups   **food processor size** 4 to 14 cups

why this recipe works In theory, the best way to guarantee a light, perfectly creamy, silky-smooth texture in hummus is to remove the chickpeas' tough skins. However, we couldn't find an approach that wasn't super-tedious or futile. Instead, we turned to the food processor. Simply pureeing the chickpeas alone gave us grainy hummus, but when we made an emulsion by blending in water and oil, we got just the light, creamy texture we were after. We started by grinding convenient canned chickpeas, then slowly added small amounts of water and lemon juice. Then we whisked the olive oil and a generous amount of tahini together and drizzled the mixture into the chickpeas while processing; this created a lush, light, and flavorful puree. Earthy cumin, garlic, and a pinch of cayenne kept the flavors balanced. The processor makes it easy to add flavorings for our variations without sacrificing the texture of the hummus.

¼ cup water

2 tablespoons lemon juice

¼ cup tahini

2 tablespoons extra-virgin olive oil, plus extra for serving

1 (15-ounce) can chickpeas, rinsed

1 garlic clove, peeled and smashed

½ teaspoon salt

¼ teaspoon ground cumin

Pinch cayenne pepper

1 Combine water and lemon juice in bowl. In separate bowl, whisk tahini and oil together until combined.

2 Process chickpeas, garlic, salt, cumin, and cayenne in food processor until coarsely ground, about 15 seconds, scraping down sides of bowl as needed. With processor running, slowly add water mixture until incorporated and process until smooth, about 1 minute. With processor running, slowly add tahini mixture until incorporated and process until creamy, about 15 seconds.

3 Transfer hummus to serving bowl, cover, and let sit until flavors meld, about 30 minutes. Drizzle with extra oil before serving. (Hummus can be refrigerated for up to 5 days. Before serving, stir in 1 tablespoon warm water to loosen hummus texture if necessary.)

LEMONY HERB HUMMUS
Add 2 tablespoons fresh mint leaves, 1 tablespoon fresh dill fronds, and ¼ teaspoon grated lemon zest to processor with chickpeas.

SPICY ROASTED RED PEPPER HUMMUS
Add ¼ cup jarred roasted red peppers, rinsed and patted dry, and ¼ teaspoon smoked paprika to processor with chickpeas. Increase cayenne to ⅛ teaspoon.

CILANTRO AND CURRY HUMMUS
Substitute lime juice for lemon juice. Add 2 tablespoons fresh cilantro and 1 teaspoon curry powder to processor with chickpeas.

ULTIMATE LAYER DIP

serves 8 to 10   **food processor size** 9 to 14 cups

why this recipe works The key to a great layer dip is ensuring that each layer has enough fresh flavor and structure to prevent the components from becoming muddled. We used the food processor to tackle all the different layers quickly and easily, infusing each with bold Southwestern flavors. To start, we made a quick salsa by processing jalapeños, cilantro, and scallions together and then added fresh tomatoes in batches, which ensured a perfect consistency. While the salsa drained (to keep the dip from becoming watery), we tackled the bottom layer of the dip. Processing canned black beans with garlic, lime juice, and chili powder gave us a hearty, flavorful base. We found that the next layer, sour cream, quickly watered down the dish. We solved that problem by blending in some pepper Jack cheese to give this layer structure. For our guacamole layer, we simply pureed avocados with lime juice and salt; the food processor gave us the ability to choose whether it came out silky smooth or pleasantly chunky. We layered the drained salsa on top along with crunchy sliced scallions for a simple but flavor-packed version of this party favorite. We like assembling this recipe in an 8-inch square baking dish so that you can see the layers; however, a large glass bowl will also work.

1 pound pepper Jack cheese, chilled

½ cup fresh cilantro leaves

¼ cup plus 2 teaspoons lime juice (3 limes)

2 jalapeño chiles, stemmed and seeded

3 scallions, white parts cut into 1-inch lengths, green parts sliced thin

Salt and pepper

2 pounds tomatoes, cored, seeded, and cut into 1-inch pieces

1 (15-ounce) can black beans, drained but not rinsed

2 garlic cloves, peeled and smashed

¾ teaspoon chili powder

1½ cups sour cream

3 avocados, halved, pitted, and each half cut into thirds

1 Using food processor fitted with shredding disk, process pepper Jack until shredded; transfer to bowl.

2 Fit now-empty processor with chopping blade and pulse cilantro, 2 tablespoons lime juice, jalapeños, scallion whites, and ⅛ teaspoon salt until finely chopped, about 4 pulses. Add half of tomatoes and pulse until chopped, about 5 pulses; transfer to bowl. Repeat with remaining tomatoes, then stir into salsa until combined. Transfer salsa to fine-mesh strainer and let drain while preparing remaining ingredients.

3 Pulse beans, garlic, chili powder, 2 teaspoons lime juice, and ⅛ teaspoon salt in again-empty processor to chunky paste, about 8 pulses, scraping down sides of bowl as needed. Transfer bean mixture to 8-inch square baking dish and spread into even layer.

4 Process sour cream and 2½ cups shredded pepper Jack in clean, dry processor until smooth, about 20 seconds. Spread sour cream mixture evenly over bean mixture and sprinkle with remaining pepper Jack.

5 Pulse avocados, remaining 2 tablespoons lime juice, and ½ teaspoon salt in again-empty processor to chunky paste, 8 to 12 pulses. Spread guacamole mixture evenly over cheese and top with salsa. Sprinkle with sliced scallion greens. Serve. (Dip can be refrigerated for up to 24 hours. Let dip sit at room temperature for 1 hour before serving.)

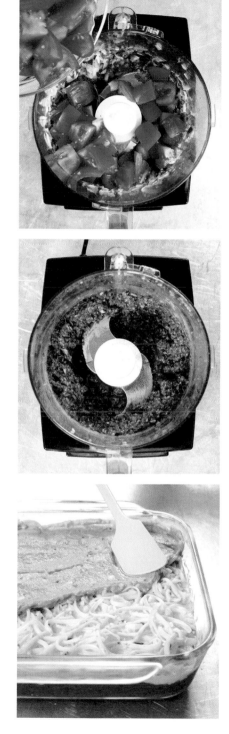

CLASSIC PESTO

makes about ¾ cup, enough for 1 pound of pasta   food processor size 4 to 14 cups

why this recipe works There are good reasons why pesto has gone from an obscure Italian sauce to an American favorite: It's incredibly delicious and, with the help of your food processor, incredibly easy. Too often, though, this bright summer sauce is overloaded with cheese and oil and bludgeoned by harsh garlic. For our recipe, we wanted to heighten the basil and subdue the garlic flavor so that all the elements would be in balance. We started with plenty of fresh basil and bruised it to release the flavorful oils. To tame the raw garlic edge, we toasted the garlic cloves. We also toasted the pine nuts to give them more intense flavor. When it comes to processing the pesto, many recipes call for adding the oil in a careful stream while the processor is running, and stirring in the cheese by hand at the last minute. We tried both, but it turned out that the pesto came out just great if we simply processed everything together at once—tasters couldn't tell the difference. With this simple, balanced recipe in hand, variations came easily. Thoroughly dry the basil leaves before processing them. You may associate pesto with pasta, but it's also good in a sandwich, on fish, spread on pizza, or stirred into soup.

3 garlic cloves, unpeeled

¼ cup pine nuts

2 cups fresh basil leaves, lightly bruised

7 tablespoons extra-virgin olive oil

¼ cup grated Parmesan cheese

Salt and pepper

1 Toast garlic in 10-inch skillet over medium heat, shaking skillet occasionally, until fragrant and skins are just beginning to brown, about 5 minutes. Add pine nuts and continue to cook until garlic is spotty brown and pine nuts are golden, 2 to 3 minutes; transfer to bowl. When cool enough to handle, peel garlic.

2 Process garlic, pine nuts, basil, oil, Parmesan, and ½ teaspoon salt in food processor until smooth, about 1 minute, scraping down sides of bowl as needed. Season with salt and pepper to taste. Serve. (Pesto can be covered with 1 tablespoon oil and refrigerated for up to 4 days or frozen for up to 1 month.)

OREGANO-LEMON PESTO

Reduce basil to 1¾ cups and substitute crumbled feta cheese for Parmesan. Add ¼ cup fresh oregano leaves, 2 tablespoons lemon juice, and ½ teaspoon grated lemon zest to processor with garlic.

SUN-DRIED TOMATO AND ARUGULA PESTO

Substitute 1 cup baby arugula and 1 cup fresh parsley leaves for basil. Add ½ cup oil-packed sun-dried tomatoes, rinsed and patted dry, to processor with garlic.

HOMEMADE MAYONNAISE

makes about ¾ cup   food processor size 4 to 14 cups

why this recipe works If you have never made your own mayonnaise, you will be surprised by just how easy it is and how much better it tastes than store-bought versions. While the traditional method of hand whisking is a bit of a balancing act as you try to pour a thin stream of oil with one hand and simultaneously whisk with the other, using a food processor requires no special dexterity, and the mayonnaise emerges silky smooth and creamy, with a rich, lush flavor. The magic behind this creaminess is the emulsion created as oil is steadily combined with egg yolks, which contain a natural emulsifier, lecithin. This first helps bind the oil and the other liquid ingredients together and then prevents them from separating, creating a uniformly creamy consistency. To make our mayo even more foolproof, we used two yolks and added another emulsifying ingredient: Dijon mustard. We found that just a bit of Dijon further emulsified the mixture and added a pleasant hint of acidity. As for our oil, we used vegetable oil for its neutral flavor, and we drizzled it very slowly into the egg-lemon-Dijon mixture while the processor was running to make sure the mixture became perfectly emulsified. To balance out the richness, extra fresh lemon juice kept this mayo bright and tangy, and a tiny amount of sugar added a hint of sweetness. For our simple variations, we turned to the strong flavors of garlic, horseradish, and smoked paprika. Smaller food processors achieved the best results in this recipe. If using a 14-cup food processor, make sure to scrape the processor bowl often during processing.

2 large egg yolks

4 teaspoons lemon juice

¼ teaspoon Dijon mustard

⅛ teaspoon sugar

Salt and pepper

¾ cup vegetable oil

Process egg yolks, lemon juice, mustard, sugar, and ¼ teaspoon salt in food processor until combined, about 10 seconds, scraping bottom and sides of bowl halfway through processing. With processor running, slowly drizzle in oil until completely emulsified, about 2 minutes. Season with salt and pepper to taste. Transfer mayonnaise to storage container. Serve. (Mayonnaise can be refrigerated for up to 3 days.)

HOMEMADE GARLICKY MAYONNAISE
Add 2 peeled and smashed garlic cloves to processor with egg yolks.

HOMEMADE HORSERADISH MAYONNAISE
Omit lemon juice. Add 3 tablespoons prepared horseradish and ¼ teaspoon pepper to processor with egg yolks.

HOMEMADE SMOKED PAPRIKA MAYONNAISE
Add 1½ teaspoons smoked paprika, ¼ teaspoon ground cumin, and 1 small garlic clove, peeled and smashed, to processor with egg yolks. Substitute lime juice for lemon juice.

PEANUT BUTTER

makes about 2 cups   food processor size 7 to 14 cups

why this recipe works Making peanut butter is so simple—dry-roasted, unsalted peanuts go into the oven for a few minutes and then into the food processor, where they are ground into a paste. Nevertheless, recipes proliferate. A surprising number call for additional ingredients like vegetable oil. The thinking seems to be that peanuts need help turning into butter, but as we tested our recipe, we found that really all you have to do is wait. With each minute the processor's metal blade whirled, more of the peanuts' oil was released, which was all we really needed to make a great home-ground nut butter. Plus, with our fingers on the button, we controlled the final texture—creamy or chunky. This is peanut butter in its purest form; no added fats, sugar, or preservatives, just a tiny bit of salt to enhance the flavor. Be aware that the ground nut mixture will appear to seize up in the food processor before turning into a smooth paste.

4 cups (1¼ pounds) dry-roasted, unsalted peanuts
Salt

1 Adjust oven rack to middle position and heat oven to 375 degrees. Spread peanuts in single layer in rimmed baking sheet and toast until fragrant and darkened slightly, 5 to 10 minutes, rotating sheet halfway through cooking. Transfer peanuts to food processor, add ½ teaspoon salt, and let cool to room temperature, about 20 minutes.

2A for creamy peanut butter Process peanuts to smooth paste, 5 to 7 minutes, scraping down sides of bowl as needed.

2B for chunky peanut butter Pulse peanuts until coarsely chopped, 3 to 5 pulses. Reserve 1 cup chopped peanuts and continue processing remaining peanuts to smooth paste, 5 to 7 minutes, scraping down sides of bowl as needed. Add chopped peanuts and pulse until combined, 3 to 5 pulses.

3 Season peanut butter with salt to taste. Transfer peanut butter to storage container. Serve. (Peanut butter can be refrigerated for up to 2 months.)

ALMOND BUTTER
Substitute 4 cups dry-roasted, unsalted almonds for peanuts.

CARAMELIZED ONION JAM

makes about 1 cup   **food processor size** 7 to 14 cups

why this recipe works Your food processor is a great shortcut to homemade preserves and jams with a texture worthy of store-bought. Caramelized onion jam is a test kitchen favorite—its savory sweetness and rich color belie its simplicity. It is quite versatile, pairing well with a wedge of cheese, as part of a sandwich, or spread on pizza. For our approachable homemade version of this jam, we started by cooking the onions with some earthy aromatics—bay leaf and rosemary—until they were golden brown. We found that covering the onions for the first 10 minutes of cooking allowed them to release some of their natural liquid without breaking down too quickly or burning. Once the onions caramelized, we stirred in balsamic vinegar, water, and sugar. After the mixture reduced for a short time, it was on its way to a jammy consistency. Processing the long onion strands in the food processor created the perfect chunky texture for all kinds of applications.

1¼ pounds onions, quartered through root end

3 tablespoons extra-virgin olive oil

1 bay leaf

1 teaspoon fresh rosemary leaves

½ teaspoon salt

¼ teaspoon pepper

2 garlic cloves, peeled and smashed

¼ cup balsamic vinegar

¼ cup water

2 tablespoons sugar

1 Working in batches, use food processor fitted with slicing disk to process onions until thinly sliced; transfer to bowl.

2 Heat oil in Dutch oven over medium-high heat until shimmering. Stir in onions, bay leaf, rosemary, salt, and pepper. Cover and cook, stirring occasionally, until onions have softened and released their liquid, about 10 minutes.

3 Stir in garlic. Reduce heat to medium-low and cook, uncovered, scraping up any browned bits, until onions are golden brown, about 15 minutes.

4 Stir in vinegar, water, and sugar, scraping up any browned bits. Increase heat to medium-high and simmer until mixture is thickened and rubber spatula or wooden spoon leaves distinct trail when dragged across bottom of pot, about 2 minutes.

5 Fit now-empty processor with chopping blade. Discard bay leaf. Transfer onion mixture to processor and pulse to jamlike consistency, about 5 pulses. Transfer jam to storage container and let cool to room temperature. Serve. (Jam can be refrigerated for up to 4 days.)

BACON JAM

makes about 1 cup   **food processor size** 7 to 14 cups

why this recipe works Pairing maple and bacon seemed like a no-brainer when it came to developing a savory jam. The first and most important step in making our bacon jam was crisping up the bacon in a Dutch oven, leaving the rendered fat behind. The rendered fat served two important purposes beyond simply being a cooking medium: First, it boosted the rich bacon flavor; and second, it gave the final jam a smooth, creamy consistency. Cooking an onion in the rendered fat allowed it to break down and take on the deep, smoky bacon flavor. Garlic and chili powder added a touch of heat, brewed coffee helped provide a roasted flavor, and cider vinegar added balance with its acidity and brightness. A good amount of maple syrup, along with brown sugar, imparted sweet, earthy notes to our jam and also helped to loosen its texture. A few pulses in the food processor chopped the jam to the perfect spreadable consistency. Bacon jam is great spread on a grilled cheese or BLT sandwich, stirred into a pasta dish, or as a component of a savory tart.

1 onion, quartered through root end

1 pound thick-cut smoked bacon, cut into 1-inch pieces

4 garlic cloves, peeled and smashed

¾ teaspoon chili powder

⅔ cup brewed coffee

⅓ cup water

¼ cup cider vinegar

¼ cup maple syrup

2 tablespoons packed brown sugar

1 Working in batches, use food processor fitted with slicing disk to process onion until thinly sliced; transfer to bowl.

2 Cook bacon in Dutch oven over medium-high heat until crisp, about 10 minutes. Using slotted spoon, transfer bacon to paper towel–lined plate.

3 Add onion to fat left in pot and cook over medium heat until softened, about 5 minutes. Stir in garlic and chili powder and cook until fragrant, about 30 seconds. Stir in bacon, coffee, water, vinegar, maple syrup, and sugar. Bring to simmer and cook, stirring occasionally, until thickened and rubber spatula or wooden spoon leaves distinct trail when dragged across bottom of pot, about 20 minutes.

4 Let bacon mixture cool for 15 minutes. Fit now-empty processor with chopping blade. Using slotted spoon, transfer bacon mixture to processor, leaving excess fat behind; discard excess fat. Pulse bacon mixture until finely chopped, 5 to 7 pulses. Transfer jam to storage container and let cool to room temperature. Serve. (Jam can be refrigerated for up to 4 days.)

SALADS & SIDES AT THE PUSH OF A BUTTON

A great side dish can be what makes the meal, but too often sides are left until the last minute and treated as an afterthought while the main dish gets all the attention. But it is precisely in these vegetable-focused dishes where the food processor shines, not only as a timesaver but also as a tool for creating consistent, evenly textured results in recipes as varied as cabbage slaw and potato gratin. We've mobilized the food processor to chop, slice, and shred a range of vegetables for sides and salads that won't feel second-class even if they take only 5 minutes to throw together.

FOOD PROCESSOR FINDINGS

Here are a few tricks we've discovered for preparing vegetables in your food processor:

1. Vegetables have a lot of liquid in them, and once they're shredded or sliced in the food processor, that liquid starts to leak out, so we frequently salt and drain prepped vegetables before cooking with them to get rid of excess moisture, which can interfere with browning. This also applies to vegetables served raw like cabbage; we salt the cabbage in our coleslaw recipe to keep it from watering down the dressing.

2. Slicing them very thinly with the food processor helps temper the bite of raw alliums like onions and shallots. We also like to let these sliced vegetable sit in an acidic vinaigrette for a little while before incorporating them into a dish, which helps even more. This trick also works for tenderizing chewy vegetables like raw mushrooms.

3. Leafy vegetables like lettuce and cabbage are easiest to process if they are in tightly packed bundles, such as hearts of romaine or quartered cabbage heads, rather than individual leaves.

ANY WAY YOU SLICE OR SHRED IT

There are many advantages to slicing and shredding vegetables in the food processor rather than by hand. First off, the processor creates much thinner, more even slices than the average home cook using a chef's knife. Thinner slices mean more net surface area, which is a boon for everything from salting the vegetables, to marinating them, to browning them during cooking. The processor-sliced vegetables cook up faster and with more flavor. Thinner, cleaner slices are also important for fibrous vegetables like celery, onions, and fennel, which can have an unpleasantly stringy texture if sliced too thick. The same is true for shredded vegetables; with uniform pieces, shredded vegetables cook up much more evenly. Of course, one of the biggest advantages is that the processor makes prep easier, safer, and much quicker.

carrots shredded in 1 minute in the food processor (left) versus in 1 minute of hand-shredding (right)

SLICED GREEN SALAD

serves 6   **food processor size** 7 to 14 cups

why this recipe works A good chopped salad offers a perfect mixture of flavors and textures in every bite, but it requires a lot of knife work to ensure that all the ingredients are evenly cut. We figured that the food processor would be the perfect tool for tackling this appealing salad without all the work. However, instead of chopping everything, we turned to the slicing blade to give us clean, even pieces of a variety of vegetables. So, after whizzing together a batch of quick, bright lemony vinaigrette, we attached the slicing disk to our food processor and thinly sliced a shallot. We let that sit in a bit of the dressing to mellow its oniony bite while we prepped the other vegetables. When it came to the base of our salad, we were surprised to see how well we could slice lettuce with the processor. In early efforts, some lettuces got stuck in the blade, spinning around under the lid without actually getting sliced, but the tightly packed leaves of hearts of romaine and compact radicchio worked wonderfully, slicing into clean, even ribbons, and we loved the texture of these short, thin shreds in the salad. For crunch and color we sliced up cucumber, radishes, and carrots, all of which took only seconds to prep in the processor. We topped our salad with cool, creamy goat cheese and nutty toasted sunflower seeds. We also developed an equally appealing Greek salad version that mixed up the flavors of the salad while keeping the method as simple and quick as possible. This recipe makes enough dressing for two to three recipes. Be sure to serve the salad immediately after tossing.

1 tablespoon mayonnaise	Salt and pepper	6 radishes, trimmed
2 tablespoons Dijon mustard	¾ cup vegetable oil	2 carrots, peeled
1 shallot, cut into 1-inch pieces	1 romaine lettuce heart, trimmed	4 ounces goat cheese, crumbled (1 cup)
3 garlic cloves, peeled and smashed	1 small head radicchio, quartered and cored	⅓ cup roasted sunflower seeds
2 teaspoons grated lemon zest plus 7 tablespoons juice (3 lemons)	½ English cucumber, halved lengthwise	

1 Process mayonnaise, mustard, shallot, garlic, lemon zest and juice, ½ teaspoon salt, and ½ teaspoon pepper in food processor until smooth, about 10 seconds, scraping down sides of bowl as needed. With processor running, slowly drizzle in oil until completely emulsified, about 2 minutes. Transfer dressing to airtight container and set aside. (Dressing can be refrigerated for up to 1 week; whisk to recombine as needed.)

2 Working in batches, process romaine, radicchio, cucumber, radishes, and carrots in now-empty processor fitted with slicing disk until thinly sliced; transfer to salad bowl. Drizzle salad with ⅓ cup dressing and gently toss to coat. Season with extra dressing, salt, and pepper to taste. Sprinkle with goat cheese and sunflower seeds. Serve immediately.

SLICED GREEK SALAD

Omit radicchio, carrots, and sunflower seeds. Substitute 1 teaspoon dried oregano and 7 tablespoons red wine vinegar for lemon zest and juice. Increase romaine to 2 heads and substitute 2 plum tomatoes, cored and halved lengthwise, for radishes, and crumbled feta cheese for goat cheese. Process ⅓ cup pitted kalamata olives with vegetables in step 2.

SHAVED MUSHROOM AND CELERY SALAD

serves 6 **food processor size** 7 to 14 cups

why this recipe works Shaved salads require the ingredients to be sliced very thin, which can be tricky, fussy work, but the food processor makes it quick and easy to get even slices of vegetables for a perfect home version of these sophisticated salads. Earthy mushrooms and crunchy celery pair well in many dishes, so we were inspired to build a shaved salad around this appealing combination. We chose cremini mushrooms for their full flavor, which would allow them to share the spotlight with assertive celery without losing their identity. To tenderize their texture without losing any of their freshness, we marinated the mushrooms in a bright lemon vinaigrette. After a quick 10-minute soak in the acidic dressing, they were both softened and nicely seasoned. The fresh celery gave our salad great crunch, and we added parsley and celery leaves for extra flavor and leafy texture. Shaved Parmesan mixed in just before serving contributed a layer of nutty, salty richness. Since getting perfectly shaved vegetables was so easy with the food processor, we also created a variation with bright, crisp fennel. If celery greens (the delicate leaves attached to the celery stalks) are not available, increase the parsley leaves to 1 cup. Make sure not to marinate the mushrooms for longer than 10 minutes; otherwise the salad will be watery.

¼ cup extra-virgin olive oil

1½ tablespoons lemon juice

Salt and pepper

8 ounces cremini mushrooms, trimmed

1 shallot, peeled

4 celery ribs, plus ½ cup celery leaves

2 ounces Parmesan cheese, shaved

½ cup fresh parsley leaves

1 Whisk oil, lemon juice, and ¼ teaspoon salt together in large bowl. Working in batches, use food processor fitted with slicing disk to process mushrooms and shallot until thinly sliced. Transfer mushrooms and shallot to bowl with dressing and toss to coat; let sit for 10 minutes.

2 Process celery in now-empty processor until thinly sliced. Add celery and leaves, Parmesan, and parsley to mushroom-shallot mixture and toss to combine. Season with salt and pepper to taste. Serve.

SHAVED MUSHROOM, FENNEL, AND ORANGE SALAD

Substitute 2 tablespoons orange juice and 1 teaspoon white wine vinegar for lemon juice and 1 fennel bulb, stalks discarded, quartered and cored, for celery.

SHAVED MUSHROOM AND CELERY SALAD WITH GOAT CHEESE AND ALMONDS

Substitute sherry vinegar for lemon juice and 1 cup crumbled goat cheese for Parmesan. Add ¼ cup toasted sliced almonds to salad before tossing in step 2.

CREAMY COLESLAW

serves 8 to 10   **food processor size** 7 to 14 cups

why this recipe works Despite its simplicity, summery coleslaw can be tough to get just right. Usually the coleslaw ends up limp and sitting in a pool of watered-down dressing. This happens because cabbage is naturally full of water; as the salad sits, that water leaches out from the chopped cabbage and dilutes the dressing. Tossing vegetables with a little salt beforehand is a simple method for drawing out excess moisture to keep the vegetables crisp and the salad creamy. Salting is more effective when there's more surface area for the salt to come in contact with, so we started by using our food processor to thinly slice the cabbage and shred the carrot and onion. As for the dressing, cutting the mayonnaise with a bit of sour cream improved the texture and added richness and a pleasant tang. We balanced plain white vinegar with a small amount of sugar for a well-rounded flavor profile. We also created two flavorful variations to increase the versatility of our slaw. For the first one, we opted for a Latin-inspired version with smoky chipotle in adobo sauce paired with cilantro and lime. For the other, we created a sweet and tangy option by switching to apple cider vinegar and adding apple and tarragon for a pop of clean, fresh flavor.

1 head green or red cabbage (2 pounds), quartered and cored

1 carrot, peeled

½ small onion, halved through root end

Salt and pepper

½ cup mayonnaise

¼ cup sour cream

1 tablespoon distilled white vinegar

2 teaspoons sugar

1 Working in batches, use food processor fitted with slicing disk to process cabbage until thinly sliced; transfer to large colander set over bowl.

2 Fit now-empty processor with shredding disk and process carrot and onion until shredded. Toss cabbage with carrot, onion, and 2 teaspoons salt in colander and let sit until wilted, at least 1 hour or up to 4 hours. Rinse cabbage mixture under cold water. Press, but do not squeeze, to drain and blot dry with paper towels. (Salted, rinsed, and dried cabbage mixture can be refrigerated in zipper-lock bag for up to 24 hours.)

3 Whisk mayonnaise, sour cream, vinegar, sugar, and ¼ teaspoon pepper together in large bowl. Add cabbage mixture and toss to coat. Refrigerate coleslaw until chilled, about 30 minutes. Season with salt and pepper to taste. Serve.

CREAMY COLESLAW WITH CHIPOTLE AND LIME
Substitute 2 tablespoons lime juice for vinegar. Add 2 tablespoons minced fresh cilantro and 2 tablespoons minced canned chipotle chile in adobo sauce to dressing.

SWEET AND TANGY COLESLAW WITH APPLE AND TARRAGON
Substitute 1 apple, peeled, cored, and halved, for onion and 2 tablespoons cider vinegar for distilled white vinegar. Increase sugar to ¼ cup and add 2 tablespoons minced fresh tarragon and 1 teaspoon Dijon mustard to dressing.

SAUTÉED SLICED BRUSSELS SPROUTS

serves 4 to 6   food processor size 7 to 14 cups

why this recipe works Brussels sprouts are delicious, but these tiny cabbages can be a huge pain to prepare by hand. While a quick-cooking method is the ideal way to get sweet, crisp-tender sprouts, they have to be thinly sliced to work in a high-heat recipe, and shredding the sprouts one by one with a knife is a laborious task. Instead, we used the food processor to power through a pound and a half of sprouts in record time. A quick soak in cold water helped keep the sprouts from burning as we sautéed them over relatively high heat. Allowing the sprouts to cook undisturbed for a few minutes also encouraged browning, which added some sweetness, and the addition of lemon juice and parsley at the end of cooking provided a shot of brightness and freshness. For variations, we turned to ingredients that went well with the caramelized profile of our sautéed Brussels sprouts. The sweet, tart flavor of cranberries complemented the sprouts' natural sweetness, and pecans helped emphasize their nuttiness and added textural interest. Our other variation used the classic pairing of Brussels sprouts with the smoky, salty crunch of bacon. Briefly soaking the shredded sprouts reduces bitterness while providing extra moisture, which helps the vegetable steam; do not skip this step.

1½ pounds Brussels sprouts, trimmed

1 tablespoon vegetable oil

Salt and pepper

2 tablespoons chopped fresh parsley

1 tablespoon lemon juice

1 Working in batches, use food processor fitted with slicing disk to process Brussels sprouts until thinly sliced. Transfer Brussels sprouts to large bowl, cover with cold water, and let sit for 3 minutes. Drain well and set aside.

2 Heat oil in 12-inch nonstick skillet over medium heat until shimmering. Add Brussels sprouts, 1 teaspoon salt, and ¼ teaspoon pepper. Cover and cook, without stirring, until Brussels sprouts are wilted and lightly browned on bottom, about 4 minutes.

3 Stir and continue to cook, uncovered, until Brussels sprouts are crisp-tender, about 3 minutes, stirring once halfway through cooking. Off heat, stir in parsley and lemon juice. Season with salt and pepper to taste. Serve.

SAUTÉED SLICED BRUSSELS SPROUTS WITH BACON

Before cooking Brussels sprouts, cook 4 slices bacon, chopped, in 12-inch nonstick skillet over medium heat until crisp, 7 to 10 minutes. Transfer bacon to paper towel–lined bowl and pour off all but 1 tablespoon fat from skillet. Cook sprouts as directed, substituting fat left in skillet for oil. Substitute cider vinegar for lemon juice and sprinkle sprouts with bacon before serving.

SAUTÉED SLICED BRUSSELS SPROUTS WITH DRIED CRANBERRIES AND PECANS

Substitute balsamic vinegar for lemon juice. Stir ½ cup dried cranberries and ½ cup toasted chopped pecans into Brussels sprouts with parsley.

CAULIFLOWER RICE

serves 4   food processor size 7 to 14 cups

why this recipe works Processed steamed cauliflower makes a surprisingly satisfying and pleas-antly fluffy substitute for rice. To make our version of this health-food trend foolproof, we first needed to figure out the best way to chop the florets to the right size. Using the food processor made quick work of breaking down the florets and created just the right grainlike texture. Working in batches helped to ensure that all of the florets broke down evenly. Next, we needed to give our neutral-tasting cauliflower a boost in flavor; a shallot and a small amount of chicken broth did the trick. To ensure that the cauliflower was tender but still maintained a pleasant, ricelike chew, we first steamed the "rice" in a covered pot, then finished cooking it uncovered to remove any remaining moisture. We also decided to develop a couple of flavorful variations so that our cauliflower rice could accompany any number of meals. This recipe can be doubled; use a Dutch oven and increase the cooking time to about 25 minutes in step 2.

1 head cauliflower (2 pounds), cored and cut into 1-inch florets

1 tablespoon extra-virgin olive oil

1 shallot, minced

½ cup chicken broth

Salt and pepper

2 tablespoons minced fresh parsley (optional)

1 Working in batches, pulse cauliflower in food processor until finely ground into ¼- to ⅛-inch pieces, 6 to 8 pulses, scraping down sides of bowl as needed; transfer to bowl.

2 Heat oil in large saucepan over medium-low heat until shimmering. Add shallot and cook until softened, about 3 minutes. Stir in processed cauliflower, broth, and 1½ teaspoons salt. Cover and cook, stirring occasionally, until cauliflower is tender, 12 to 15 minutes.

3 Uncover and continue to cook until cauliflower rice is almost completely dry, about 3 minutes. Off heat, stir in parsley, if using, and season with salt and pepper to taste.

CURRIED CAULIFLOWER RICE
Add ¼ teaspoon ground cardamom, ¼ teaspoon ground cinnamon, and ¼ teaspoon ground turmeric to saucepan with shallot. Substitute 1 tablespoon minced fresh mint for parsley and stir ¼ cup toasted sliced almonds into cauliflower rice with mint.

TEX-MEX CAULIFLOWER RICE
Add 1 minced garlic clove, 1 teaspoon ground cumin, and 1 teaspoon ground coriander to saucepan with shallot. Substitute 2 tablespoons minced fresh cilantro for parsley and stir 1 teaspoon lime juice into cauliflower rice with cilantro.

PUREED BUTTERNUT SQUASH

serves 4 to 6   food processor size 7 to 14 cups

why this recipe works For a versatile side dish that went beyond the usual mashed potatoes, we turned to sweet, earthy butternut squash. After testing various cooking methods, including roasting, steaming, braising, and microwaving, we found that the microwave worked best. Not only was it one of the easiest cooking methods, but tasters far preferred the clean, sweet squash flavor that the microwave produced. All we had to do after microwaving the squash was drain the liquid that was released during cooking and then move the whole operation to the food processor. In just seconds, the processor gave us a perfectly silky-smooth texture. Plus we found that the drained pureed squash needed only 2 tablespoons of half-and-half and 2 tablespoons of butter to round out its flavor and add some richness for a seriously simple and crowd-pleasing side dish.

2 pounds butternut squash, peeled, seeded, and cut into 1-inch pieces (6 cups)

2 tablespoons half-and-half

2 tablespoons unsalted butter

1 tablespoon packed brown sugar

Salt and pepper

1 Microwave squash in covered bowl until tender and easily pierced with fork, 15 to 20 minutes, stirring halfway through cooking.

2 Transfer squash to food processor. Add half-and-half, butter, sugar, and 1 teaspoon salt and process until squash is smooth, about 20 seconds, scraping down sides of bowl as needed. Adjust consistency with hot water as needed. Season with salt and pepper to taste. Serve.

PUREED BUTTERNUT SQUASH WITH WARM SPICES AND WALNUTS

Toss squash with ¼ teaspoon ground cumin, ¼ teaspoon ground coriander, and ⅛ teaspoon ground cinnamon before microwaving. Stir ¼ cup toasted chopped walnuts into squash before serving.

PUREED BUTTERNUT SQUASH WITH SAGE AND ALMONDS

Add 2 teaspoons minced fresh sage to processor with half-and-half. Stir ¼ cup toasted sliced almonds into squash before serving.

SAUTÉED ZUCCHINI WITH LEMON AND HERBS

serves 4   food processor size 7 to 14 cups

why this recipe works Because zucchini and summer squash are watery vegetables, they often cook up soggy and bland. We wanted to find a way to make sautéed zucchini or summer squash with concentrated flavor and an appealing texture. The key to avoiding sogginess was to remove as much water as possible before cooking the squash. We started by slicing the squash into thin pieces with the food processor, then salted the slices, drained them, and patted them dry. We also quickly sliced up and sautéed an onion to build depth in the dish before adding the drained squash along with some lemon zest. The squash became tender and lightly browned with minimal stirring. A little lemon juice and fresh basil stirred in off the heat lent bright flavors. For one variation, we combined the earthy, subtle sweetness of oregano with the briny, bright flavor of olives to complement the sautéed vegetable's freshness. In another, we added richness to the dish with crisped pancetta. Salting causes the zucchini rounds to release excess water. This important extra step helps the zucchini to sauté rather than stew in its own juice. Do not add more salt when cooking, or the dish will be too salty.

3 zucchini or yellow summer squash (8 ounces each), trimmed

Kosher salt and pepper

1 small onion, quartered through root end

3 tablespoons extra-virgin olive oil

1 teaspoon grated lemon zest plus 1 tablespoon juice

2 tablespoons minced fresh basil, parsley, and/or thyme

1 Working in batches, use food processor fitted with slicing disk to process zucchini until thinly sliced; transfer to colander set over bowl. Toss zucchini with 1 tablespoon salt in colander and let drain until roughly ⅓ cup water is released, about 30 minutes. Process onion in now-empty processor until thinly sliced; set aside. Pat zucchini dry with paper towels and carefully wipe away any residual salt.

2 Heat oil in 12-inch nonstick skillet over medium heat until shimmering. Add onion and cook until softened, about 5 minutes. Increase heat to medium-high, add zucchini and lemon zest, and cook, stirring occasionally, until zucchini is golden brown, 6 to 8 minutes. Off heat, stir in lemon juice and basil and season with pepper to taste. Serve.

SAUTÉED ZUCCHINI WITH OLIVES AND OREGANO

Substitute 1 teaspoon minced fresh oregano for basil. Add ¼ cup chopped pitted kalamata olives to zucchini with lemon juice.

SAUTÉED ZUCCHINI WITH PANCETTA AND HERBS

Before cooking onion and zucchini, cook 2 ounces finely chopped pancetta in 12-inch nonstick skillet over medium heat until crisp, 5 to 7 minutes. Transfer pancetta to paper towel–lined bowl. Cook onion and zucchini as directed, substituting fat left in skillet for oil.

CRISPY POTATO LATKES

serves 4 to 6   food processor size 7 to 14 cups

why this recipe works Fried potatoes are great in all their forms, and latkes are arguably the culmination of everything we love about this cooking method for this ingredient, with a supercrisp outer shell and buttery-soft interior. Using the shredding disk of the food processor instead of a box grater let us prepare 2 pounds of potatoes in no time and kept our knuckles safe and sound. For latkes that were light and not greasy, with creamy interiors surrounded by a shatteringly crisp outer layer, we needed to do two things: First, we removed as much water as possible from the potato shreds by wringing them out in a dish towel. Then we briefly microwaved them. This caused the starches in the potatoes to form a gel that held onto the potatoes' moisture so it didn't leach out during cooking. We also took the starch that drained out with the water and added it back to the potato mixture. The extra starch gave us the supercrisp results we were looking for. Without excess moisture, the latkes crisped up quickly and absorbed minimal oil when we fried them. Serve the latkes with applesauce and sour cream.

2 pounds russet potatoes, unpeeled

1 onion, quartered through root end

Salt and pepper

2 large eggs

2 teaspoons minced fresh parsley

Vegetable oil

1 Adjust oven rack to middle position and heat oven to 200 degrees. Working in batches, use food processor fitted with shredding disk to process potatoes and onion until shredded; transfer to large bowl. Toss potatoes and onion with 1 teaspoon salt. Place half of potato mixture in center of dish towel. Gather ends together and twist tightly to drain as much liquid as possible, reserving drained liquid in bowl. Repeat with remaining potato mixture. Transfer drained potatoes to clean bowl.

2 Cover potato mixture and microwave until just warmed through but not hot, 1 to 2 minutes, stirring with fork every 30 seconds. Spread potato mixture in rimmed baking sheet and let cool for 10 minutes; return to bowl.

3 Meanwhile, let bowl of drained potato liquid sit for 5 minutes so that starch can settle to bottom. Pour off liquid, leaving starch in bowl. Whisk eggs into starch until smooth. Add starch-egg mixture, parsley, and ¼ teaspoon pepper to cooled potato mixture and toss gently to combine.

4 Add oil to 12-inch skillet until it measures ¼ inch deep. Heat oil over medium-high heat until shimmering but not smoking (about 350 degrees). Set wire rack in rimmed baking sheet and line with triple layer of paper towels.

5 Using ¼ cup potato mixture per latke, measure 5 latkes into hot skillet, pressing each into ⅓-inch-thick pancake. Cook, adjusting heat so fat bubbles around latkes edges, until golden brown on bottom, about 3 minutes. Turn and continue cooking until golden brown on second side, about 3 minutes longer.

6 Transfer latkes to prepared sheet and keep warm in oven. Repeat with remaining potato mixture, adding oil as needed to maintain ¼-inch depth and returning oil to 350 degrees between batches. Season latkes with salt and pepper to taste. Serve.

SCALLOPED POTATOES

serves 4 to 6   **food processor size** 7 to 14 cups

why this recipe works Creamy scalloped potatoes make an elegant side dish, but because of their labor-intensive preparation and richness, they are usually relegated to indulgent holiday feasts. We wanted a lighter, quicker version that we could make for weeknight dinners, so naturally we turned to the food processor. The slicing disk cut both the potatoes and onion into thin pieces that melded into perfect layers in the oven. For a lighter take on the rich, creamy sauce, we cut heavy cream with an equal amount of chicken broth. We parboiled the sliced potatoes in the broth-and-cream combination, then poured the mixture into a casserole dish and baked it in the oven. The final touch was a sprinkling of cheddar cheese on top, which browned as the dish baked and formed a nice gooey crust. Prepare all of the other ingredients before slicing the potatoes or they will begin to brown (do not store them in water; this will make the dish bland and watery). If the potato slices do start to discolor, put them in a bowl and cover with the cream and chicken broth. You can substitute Parmesan for the cheddar, if desired.

4 ounces cheddar cheese, chilled

2 pounds russet potatoes, peeled

1 onion, quartered through root end

2 tablespoons unsalted butter

1 tablespoon minced fresh thyme or 1 teaspoon dried

2 garlic cloves, minced

Salt and pepper

1 cup chicken broth

1 cup heavy cream

2 bay leaves

1 Adjust oven rack to middle position and heat oven to 425 degrees. Grease 8-inch square baking dish.

2 Using food processor fitted with shredding disk, process cheddar until shredded; set aside. Fit now-empty processor with slicing disk. Working in batches, process potatoes until thinly sliced; set aside. Process onion in again-empty processor until thinly sliced.

3 Melt butter in Dutch oven over medium-high heat. Add onion and cook until softened, about 5 minutes. Stir in thyme, garlic, 1¼ teaspoons salt, and ¼ teaspoon pepper and cook until fragrant, about 30 seconds.

4 Add potatoes, broth, cream, and bay leaves and bring to simmer. Cover, reduce heat to medium-low, and simmer until potatoes are almost tender (paring knife can be slipped in and out of potato slice with some resistance), about 10 minutes.

5 Discard bay leaves. Transfer mixture to prepared dish and press into even layer. Sprinkle evenly with cheddar and bake until bubbling around edges and top is golden brown, about 15 minutes. Let casserole cool for at least 15 minutes before serving.

THICK-CUT POTATO CHIPS

makes 7 cups food processor size 7 to 14 cups

why this recipe works Stop settling for greasy, oversalted store-bought options: Making fresh, crisp, addictive potato chips at home is not as hard as you think, and with the help of your food processor, the prep is a cinch. There's more to making great chips than just slicing potatoes and frying them, though. The thickness of the potato slices is the first important element. We chose Yukon Gold potatoes for their great potato flavor, and the food processor gave us perfectly even and consistent ⅛-inch slices, which were thick enough to hold their shape during frying, yet thin enough to cook up crisp and crunchy. The frying technique took a little work. On our first attempts, we got dark brown, bitter chips. We soon realized that the amount of starch in the potatoes was the source of our troubles, which led us to a method of rinsing, parboiling, and then frying. Rinsing washed away the exterior starch, and parboiling jump-started the cooking and further reduced the amount of starch in the potatoes. Frying the potatoes in batches ensured that the oil temperature didn't drop too much and that the chips did not turn out greasy. It was a bit of extra work, but the reward of fresh, golden homemade potato chips was well worth it. These chips taste great with just a little salt sprinkled on them, but for fans of flavored potato chips, we also created buttermilk ranch and barbecue options. Use a Dutch oven that holds 6 quarts or more. These chips are best enjoyed the day they are made.

2 pounds Yukon Gold potatoes, unpeeled

2 quarts vegetable oil

Kosher salt and pepper

1 Working in batches, use food processor fitted with slicing disk to process potatoes until thinly sliced; transfer to large bowl. Cover potatoes with cold water and gently swirl to rinse off starch. Drain potatoes and repeat swirling with cold water until water no longer turns cloudy, about 5 rinses.

2 Line rimmed baking sheet with clean dish towel. Bring 2 quarts water to boil in large saucepan over high heat. Add potatoes, return to simmer, and cook until just beginning to soften, about 3 minutes. Gently drain potatoes and spread into even layer in prepared sheet. Top with another clean dish towel and press gently on potatoes to dry thoroughly.

3 Set wire rack in rimmed baking sheet and line with triple layer of paper towels. Add oil to large Dutch oven until it measures about 1½ inches deep and heat over medium-high heat to 350 degrees. Carefully add one-third of potatoes to oil and fry, stirring frequently to separate chips, until golden and crisp, 12 to 18 minutes. Adjust burner, if necessary, to maintain oil temperature of about 325 degrees. Using

skimmer or slotted spoon, transfer chips to prepared sheet as they finish cooking and season with salt and pepper to taste. Let chips cool completely. Return oil to 350 degrees and repeat with remaining potatoes in 2 batches. Serve.

THICK-CUT RANCH POTATO CHIPS
Whisk 1 tablespoon kosher salt, 1 tablespoon buttermilk powder, 2 teaspoons dried dill weed, ¼ teaspoon garlic powder, and ¼ teaspoon onion powder together in bowl. Gently toss each batch of chips with one-third of ranch seasoning before transferring to prepared rack to cool.

THICK-CUT BARBECUE POTATO CHIPS
Whisk 1 tablespoon kosher salt, 1 tablespoon packed brown sugar, 2 teaspoons smoked paprika, 1 teaspoon garlic powder, and ⅛ teaspoon cayenne pepper together in bowl. Gently toss each batch of chips with one-third of barbecue seasoning before transferring to prepared rack to cool.

QUICK PICKLE CHIPS

makes 2 cups   **food processor size** 7 to 14 cups

why this recipe works A snap to make, these quick-pickled cucumber slices are an approachable fuss-free pickle for a novice or a great go-to recipe for anyone looking to satisfy a craving without the effort involved in larger-scale pickling projects. Just a few easy steps transform a handful of cucumbers into perfect pickle chips—crunchy, tangy, a bit sweet, and loaded with fresh, aromatic flavor. Like a classic bread-and-butter pickle, these chips get a hint of warm spice from black peppercorns, mustard seeds, and turmeric. Fresh dill sprigs add a mild anise flavor, befitting a hamburger pickle. To streamline our preparation time, we chose seasoned rice vinegar—which contains vinegar, sugar, and salt—and eliminated the work of separately measuring three ingredients. The slicing disk of the food processor made quick work of our cucumbers, producing perfectly cut chips in minutes. We heated our glass jar in hot water to ensure that it wouldn't crack when we filled it with hot brine. After 3 hours, these pickles were thoroughly suffused with a lively combination of sweet, sour, and aromatic tones. This quick-pickling method also worked great for other firm vegetables like fennel and carrots in our simple variations. Be sure to choose the freshest, firmest pickling cucumbers available, for guaranteed crunch. These pickles can be refrigerated for up to 6 weeks; they will soften significantly after 6 weeks.

8 ounces pickling cucumbers, trimmed

¾ cup seasoned rice vinegar

¼ cup water

1 garlic clove, peeled and halved

¼ teaspoon ground turmeric

⅛ teaspoon black peppercorns

⅛ teaspoon yellow mustard seeds

2 sprigs fresh dill

1 Working in batches, use food processor fitted with slicing disk to process cucumbers until thinly sliced; set aside.

2 Bring vinegar, water, garlic, turmeric, peppercorns, and mustard seeds to boil in medium saucepan over medium-high heat.

3 Meanwhile, place one 1-pint jar under hot running water until heated through, about 1 minute; shake dry. Pack cucumbers and dill into hot jar. Using funnel and ladle, pour hot brine over cucumbers to cover. Let jar cool to room temperature, about 30 minutes. Cover jar with lid and refrigerate for at least 2½ hours before serving.

QUICK PICKLED FENNEL
Omit dill. Substitute 1 fennel bulb (12 ounces), stalks discarded, quartered and cored, for cucumber and fennel seeds for turmeric.

QUICK PICKLED CARROTS
Omit turmeric. Substitute 8 ounces carrots, peeled, for cucumber and fresh tarragon for dill.

CHOP & SLICE YOUR WAY TO MEATLESS MAINS

While we definitely think that home cooks should develop their knife skills, we can all use a little assist in the ingredient prep stage of a recipe, especially when we have to chop, dice, slice, and/or shred our way through a laundry list of components. The detailed lineup of ingredients in many vegetable-centric main dishes can make these recipes seem intimidating, and often different vegetables need to be prepared in different ways. The following set of some of our favorite meatless mains permits you to put down the knife (and the mandoline and the grater) and let your food processor be your prep cook. You'll get more uniform results while saving time, energy, and your sanity.

FOOD PROCESSOR FINDINGS

Here are a few tricks we've discovered for making meatless mains easier in the food processor:

1 With the processor running, prepping two kinds of vegetables is almost as easy as prepping one, which opens the door to combining multiple veggies in new and interesting ways, as in our Celery Root and Potato Roesti (page 65).

2 The food processor is a secret weapon for multipart dishes—it brings both dough and filling together in seconds for a quiche or vegetarian pot pie or quickly slices all the vegetables and makes the sauce for a stir-fry.

3 Adding a homemade sauce or topping to jazz up a simple weeknight dish takes almost no extra work when you use the food processor, whether it's an herbal *pistou* for our Provençal Vegetable Soup (page 79) or a cooling cucumber-yogurt sauce to pair with our flavorful Chickpea Cakes (page 62).

4 Grinding your own burgers isn't just for meat—we found just the right pulsing technique to make stellar bean and chickpea patties that held together but kept a great chunky texture.

MORE THAN JUST A PRETTY PLATE

Ingredients that are cut into clean, even pieces produce more attractive final results, but it's not all about looks. Using your food processor to ensure evenly sliced carrots and minced garlic also helps make sure that your ingredients cook at an even rate. This is especially important in quick-cooking, high-heat dishes like a stir-fry where uneven pieces will burn if they are too small or remain raw if they are too large. It's also key for recipes with a lot of ingredients, like a soup, where you want to make sure every bite has a mixture of flavors and ingredients that are all fully cooked through. Dishes that contain several types of vegetables feel more balanced when everything has a similar shape and is cooked evenly.

hand-sliced zucchini, yellow summer squash, and tomatoes

zucchini, yellow summer squash, and tomatoes sliced in the food processor

BLACK BEAN BURGERS

serves 6   food processor size 7 to 14 cups

why this recipe works Black beans make the perfect base for a flavorful vegetarian burger. A good black bean burger rides the line between being dry and falling apart and being gluey and mushy. By pulsing the beans to a rough chop, we allowed them to maintain good texture. The challenge, then, was to bind them into a cohesive mixture without drying it out or compromising the flavor. The key proved to be grinding tortilla chips in the food processor to use as a binder rather than bread crumbs. Eggs and a little flour also helped to hold the burger mixture together. To give the burgers some much-needed personality, we opted for a Latin American profile. Garlic, scallions, and fresh cilantro chopped fine in the processor provided a quick and easy boost in flavor. Citrusy coriander and smoky cumin added more complexity, and a dash of hot sauce added zip, as did our quick chipotle mayo sauce. Letting the mixture sit in the refrigerator for an hour gave the starches time to soak up moisture from the eggs, so the patties were easier to shape.

sauce

3 tablespoons mayonnaise

3 tablespoons sour cream

2 teaspoons minced canned chipotle chile in adobo sauce

1 garlic clove, minced

⅛ teaspoon salt

burgers

2 (15-ounce) cans black beans, rinsed

1 ounce tortilla chips, crushed (½ cup)

4 scallions, cut into 1-inch lengths

½ cup fresh cilantro leaves

2 garlic cloves, peeled and smashed

2 large eggs

2 tablespoons all-purpose flour

1 teaspoon ground cumin

1 teaspoon hot sauce

½ teaspoon ground coriander

¼ teaspoon salt

¼ teaspoon pepper

¼ cup vegetable oil

6 hamburger buns

1 for the sauce Combine all ingredients in bowl and refrigerate until ready to serve.

2 for the burgers Line rimmed baking sheet with triple layer of paper towels and spread beans over towels. Let sit for 15 minutes.

3 Process tortilla chips in food processor until finely ground, about 30 seconds. Add scallions, cilantro, and garlic and pulse until finely chopped, about 15 pulses, scraping down sides of bowl as needed. Add beans and pulse until beans are roughly broken down, about 5 pulses.

4 Whisk eggs, flour, cumin, hot sauce, coriander, salt, and pepper together in large bowl until well combined. Add bean mixture and mix until just combined. Cover and refrigerate for at least 1 hour or up to 24 hours.

5 Adjust oven rack to middle position and heat oven to 200 degrees. Set wire rack in rimmed baking sheet. Divide bean mixture into 6 equal portions. Firmly pack each portion into tight ball, then flatten to 3½-inch-wide burgers.

6 Heat 1 tablespoon oil in 12-inch nonstick skillet over medium heat until shimmering. Carefully place 3 burgers in skillet and cook until bottoms are well browned and crisp, about 5 minutes. Flip burgers, add 1 tablespoon oil, and cook second side until well browned and crisp, 3 to 5 minutes. Transfer burgers to prepared rack and keep warm in oven. Repeat with remaining 3 patties and remaining 2 tablespoons oil. Transfer burgers to buns and serve with sauce.

CHICKPEA CAKES WITH CUCUMBER-YOGURT SAUCE

serves 6   food processor size 7 to 14 cups

why this recipe works For a vegetarian patty that was filling but light, we turned to hearty chickpeas paired with fresh flavors. We did hit some challenges when it came to finding the right texture, however. If underprocessed, the beans didn't hold together; if overprocessed, they became hummus. We settled on pulsing the beans just a few times to get a mixture of finely chopped chickpeas and larger pieces, a trick we'd learned from making other home-ground burgers. We also added two eggs and some panko bread crumbs as a neutral-tasting binder, and yogurt and olive oil for richness. Garam masala, cayenne pepper, scallions, and cilantro gave the patties a flavorful kick, and a cooling yogurt sauce with shredded cucumber brightened the dish. Avoid overworking the chickpea mixture or the cakes will have a mealy texture. Serve with lime wedges.

sauce

1 cucumber, peeled, halved lengthwise, and seeded

1 cup plain Greek yogurt

2 tablespoons extra-virgin olive oil

¼ cup minced fresh cilantro, parsley, or mint

1 garlic clove, minced

Salt and pepper

cakes

2 (15-ounce) cans chickpeas, rinsed

¼ cup fresh cilantro leaves

2 scallions, cut into 1-inch lengths

1 shallot, cut into 1-inch pieces

2 large eggs

⅓ cup plain Greek yogurt

6 tablespoons extra-virgin olive oil

1 teaspoon garam masala

⅛ teaspoon cayenne pepper

⅛ teaspoon salt

1 cup panko bread crumbs

1 for the sauce Using food processor fitted with shredding disk, process cucumber until shredded. Whisk yogurt, oil, cilantro, and garlic together in medium bowl. Stir in cucumber and season with salt and pepper to taste; refrigerate until ready to serve.

2 for the cakes Line rimmed baking sheet with triple layer of paper towels and spread chickpeas over towels. Let sit for 15 minutes.

3 Fit now-empty processor with chopping blade and pulse cilantro, scallions, and shallot until finely chopped, about 15 pulses, scraping down sides of bowl as needed. Add chickpeas and pulse until chickpeas are roughly broken down, about 5 pulses.

4 Whisk eggs, yogurt, 2 tablespoons oil, garam masala, cayenne, and salt together in large bowl. Add chickpea mixture and panko and mix until just combined. Cover and refrigerate for at least 1 hour or up to 24 hours.

5 Adjust oven rack to middle position and heat oven to 200 degrees. Set wire rack in rimmed baking sheet. Divide chickpea mixture into 6 equal portions. Gently pack each portion into ball, then flatten to 3½-inch-wide patty.

6 Heat 1 tablespoon oil in 12-inch nonstick skillet over medium heat until shimmering. Carefully place 3 patties in skillet. Cook until bottoms are well browned and crisp, about 5 minutes. Flip patties, add 1 tablespoon oil, and cook second side until well browned and crisp, 3 to 5 minutes. Transfer patties to prepared rack and keep warm in oven. Repeat with remaining 3 patties and remaining 2 tablespoons oil. Serve with sauce.

CELERY ROOT AND POTATO ROESTI WITH LEMON-PARSLEY CRÈME FRAÎCHE

serves 2 to 3 **food processor size** 7 to 14 cups

why this recipe works Hugely popular in Switzerland, *roesti* is a large golden-brown pancake of simply seasoned grated potatoes fried in butter. We set out to master the crunchy, crisp exterior and tender, creamy interior of this recipe while also revitalizing the flavors and simplifying the prep. In order to produce a cake with a decidedly fresh flavor, we swapped out some of the potatoes for celery root, which gave our roesti a brighter profile. The food processor shredded both root vegetables in just seconds. Producing a golden-brown crust was easy, but the inside of the roesti came out gluey and half-cooked. To solve these problems we eliminated excess moisture by salting our vegetables, then wringing them dry in a dish towel. To ensure that our potato cake held together, we tossed the potatoes and celery root with a small amount of cornstarch. Creating a rich but bright sauce to accompany our roesti was as simple as combining tangy crème fraîche with parsley and lemon zest and juice. For a distinctive variation, we replaced the celery root with beets and simply tweaked the seasoning and our sauce to match that sweeter, earthier vegetable. The processor shredded the beets without the usual stained fingers and cutting board.

¼ cup crème fraîche	Salt and pepper	2 teaspoons cornstarch
3 tablespoons minced fresh parsley	1 pound russet potatoes, peeled	4 tablespoons unsalted butter
2½ teaspoons grated lemon zest plus ½ teaspoon juice	1 celery root (14 ounces), peeled and quartered	

1 Combine crème fraîche, 1 tablespoon parsley, ½ teaspoon lemon zest, lemon juice, and ⅛ teaspoon salt in bowl; refrigerate until ready to serve.

2 Working in batches, use food processor fitted with shredding disk to process potatoes and celery root until shredded. Toss potatoes and celery root with ¾ teaspoon salt in colander and let drain for 30 minutes.

3 Working in 3 batches, place shredded potato mixture in center of dish towel. Gather ends together and twist tightly to drain as much liquid as possible, discarding liquid; transfer drained potato mixture to large bowl. Add cornstarch, ¼ teaspoon pepper, remaining 2 tablespoons parsley, and remaining 2 teaspoons lemon zest and toss to combine.

4 Melt 2 tablespoons butter in 10-inch nonstick skillet over medium-low heat. Add potato mixture and spread into even layer. Cover and cook for 5 minutes. Uncover and, using greased spatula, gently press potato mixture to form compact, round cake. Cook, pressing on cake occasionally, until bottom is deep golden brown, about 10 minutes.

5 Run spatula around edge of skillet and shake skillet to loosen roesti; slide onto large plate. Melt remaining 2 tablespoons butter in now-empty skillet. Invert roesti onto second plate, then slide it, browned side up, back into skillet. Cook, pressing on cake occasionally, until bottom is well browned, about 15 minutes. Transfer roesti to wire rack and let cool for 5 minutes. Cut into wedges and serve with sauce.

BEET AND POTATO ROESTI WITH ORANGE-CHIVE CRÈME FRAÎCHE

Substitute chives for parsley, orange zest and juice for lemon zest and juice, and 1 pound beets, peeled and quartered, for celery root.

66 • FOOD PROCESSOR PERFECTION

SUMMER VEGETABLE GRATIN

serves 4   **food processor size** 7 to 14 cups

why this recipe works   The thought of a rich gratin showcasing all our favorite summer vegetables was very appealing, as was the idea of using the food processor to make prepping all the different vegetables a breeze. Unfortunately, every version we tried ended up a soggy mess thanks to the liquid the vegetables released. To fix this problem, we salted the sliced zucchini, summer squash, and tomatoes and let them drain before assembling the casserole. We also baked the dish uncovered so that the remaining excess moisture would evaporate in the oven. To flavor the vegetables, we tossed them with thyme-infused olive oil and then drizzled more oil over the top of the dish. Fresh bread crumbs (also made in the food processor) tossed with Parmesan and garlic made an elegant topping. The success of this recipe depends on high-quality vegetables. Buy zucchini and summer squash of roughly the same diameter. We like the combination, but you can also use just zucchini or just summer squash.

2 zucchini (8 ounces each), trimmed

2 yellow summer squash (8 ounces each), trimmed

Salt and pepper

1½ pounds ripe but firm plum tomatoes, cored

2 onions, quartered through root end

6 tablespoons extra-virgin olive oil

1 slice hearty white sandwich bread, torn into quarters

2 garlic cloves, peeled and smashed

2 ounces Parmesan cheese, grated (1 cup)

1 tablespoon minced fresh thyme

¼ cup chopped fresh basil

1 Working in batches, use food processor fitted with slicing disk to process zucchini and summer squash until thinly sliced. Toss zucchini and summer squash with 1 teaspoon salt in colander and let sit until vegetables release at least 3 tablespoons liquid, about 45 minutes. Pat zucchini and summer squash dry firmly with paper towels, removing as much liquid as possible.

2 Meanwhile, process tomatoes in now-empty processor until thinly sliced. Spread tomatoes on paper towel–lined baking sheets, sprinkle with ½ teaspoon salt, and let sit for 30 minutes. Thoroughly pat tomatoes dry with more paper towels.

3 Process onions in again-empty processor until thinly sliced. Heat 1 tablespoon oil in 12-inch nonstick skillet over medium heat until shimmering. Add onions and ½ teaspoon salt and cook, stirring occasionally, until softened and dark golden brown, 20 to 25 minutes; set aside.

4 Fit again-empty processor with chopping blade and pulse bread and garlic until finely chopped, about 10 pulses. Combine bread-crumb mixture, Parmesan, and 1 tablespoon oil in bowl. Combine 3 tablespoons oil, thyme, and ½ teaspoon pepper in separate bowl.

5 Adjust oven rack to upper-middle position and heat oven to 400 degrees. Grease 3-quart gratin dish (or 13 by 9-inch baking dish) with remaining 1 tablespoon oil. Toss zucchini and summer squash with half of thyme-oil mixture and arrange in prepared dish. Sprinkle evenly with caramelized onions, then top with tomato slices, overlapping them slightly. Spoon remaining thyme-oil mixture evenly over tomatoes. Bake until vegetables are tender and tomatoes are starting to brown on edges, 40 to 45 minutes.

6 Remove baking dish from oven and increase heat to 450 degrees. Sprinkle bread crumb–mixture evenly over gratin and bake until bubbling and cheese is lightly browned, 5 to 10 minutes. Let cool for 10 minutes, then sprinkle with basil. Serve.

VEGETABLE POT PIE

serves 4 to 6   **food processor size** 7 to 14 cups

why this recipe works We wanted a from-scratch vegetable pot pie that featured flavorful gravy, a flaky, tender crust, and plenty of hearty vegetables, and we wanted to do as much of the prep work as possible in the food processor. We started by creating a pie dough in the processor, which made quick work of cutting the butter into the flour. When it came to the vegetables, we chose mushrooms, sweet potatoes, and turnips, all of which had the ability to withstand a longer cooking time without losing their integrity. The food processor gave us thin, uniform slices of each vegetable, which ensured that everything cooked evenly. We quickly sautéed the sliced vegetables before stirring in handfuls of tender spinach for the last couple of minutes of cooking. We used the flavorful fond left over after the sautéing step to build our savory gravy. A final sprinkling of Parmesan and a splash of lemon juice enhanced the flavor of the filling before we topped the pot pie with our buttery crust and put the whole thing in the oven to bake.

crust

3 tablespoons ice water, plus extra as needed

4 teaspoons sour cream

1¼ cups (6¼ ounces) all-purpose flour

1½ teaspoons sugar

½ teaspoon salt

8 tablespoons unsalted butter, cut into ¼-inch pieces and frozen for 10 to 15 minutes

filling

1 sweet potato, peeled and quartered lengthwise

8 ounces turnips, peeled and quartered

1 onion, quartered through root end

8 ounces cremini mushrooms, trimmed

4 tablespoons unsalted butter

Salt and pepper

3 garlic cloves, minced

½ teaspoon grated lemon zest, plus 1 tablespoon juice

8 ounces curly-leaf spinach, stemmed

2 tablespoons all-purpose flour

2 cups vegetable broth

1 ounce Parmesan cheese, grated (½ cup)

2 tablespoons minced fresh parsley

1 large egg, lightly beaten with 1 teaspoon water and pinch salt

1 for the crust Whisk ice water and sour cream together in bowl. Process flour, sugar, and salt in food processor until combined, about 3 seconds. Scatter frozen butter over top and pulse mixture until butter is size of large peas, about 10 pulses.

2 Pour half of sour cream mixture over flour mixture and pulse until incorporated, about 3 pulses. Repeat with remaining sour cream mixture. Pinch dough with your fingers; if dough feels dry and does not hold together, sprinkle 1 to 2 tablespoons more ice water over mixture and pulse until dough forms large clumps and no dry flour remains, 3 to 5 pulses.

3 Turn dough onto sheet of plastic wrap and flatten into 4-inch disk. Wrap tightly and refrigerate for 1 hour. Before rolling out dough, let it sit on counter to soften slightly, about 10 minutes. (Dough can be refrigerated for up to 2 days or frozen for up to 1 month. If frozen, let dough thaw completely on counter before rolling it out.)

4 Roll dough between 2 large sheets of parchment paper into 10-inch circle. (If dough is soft and/or sticky, refrigerate until firm.) Remove parchment on top of dough. Fold outer ½ inch of dough toward center, then crimp into tidy, fluted edge using fingers. Using paring knife, cut four 2-inch oval-shaped vents in center. Slide parchment paper with crust onto baking sheet and refrigerate until needed.

5 for the filling Adjust oven rack to middle position and heat oven to 400 degrees. Working in batches, use clean, dry processor fitted with slicing disk to process potato and turnips until thinly sliced; set aside. Process onion and mushrooms in now-empty processor until thinly sliced.

6 Melt 2 tablespoons butter in Dutch oven over medium heat. Add onion, mushrooms, and ½ teaspoon salt and cook until mushrooms have released their liquid, about 5 minutes. Add potato and turnips, cover, and cook, stirring occasionally, until potato and turnips begin to soften around edges, 5 to 7 minutes. Stir in garlic and lemon zest and cook until fragrant, about 30 seconds. Stir in spinach, 1 handful at a time, and cook until wilted, about 2 minutes. Transfer filling to bowl.

7 Melt remaining 2 tablespoons butter in now-empty pot over medium-high heat. Stir in flour and cook for 1 minute. Gradually whisk in broth, scraping up any browned bits and smoothing out any lumps. Bring to simmer and cook until sauce thickens slightly, about 1 minute. Off heat, whisk in Parmesan, parsley, lemon juice, and ½ teaspoon salt. Stir in vegetable mixture and any accumulated juices and season with salt and pepper to taste.

8 Transfer filling to 9½-inch deep-dish pie plate set in aluminum foil–lined rimmed baking sheet. Place chilled crust on top and brush with egg mixture. Bake until crust is golden brown and filling is bubbling, about 30 minutes. Let cool for 10 minutes before serving.

QUICHE WITH LEEKS AND GOAT CHEESE

serves 6 to 8   food processor size 7 to 14 cups

why this recipe works Perfect quiche should feature velvety-smooth custard enveloped in a buttery, flaky pastry. To create a tender crust without doing lots of work by hand, we used the food processor, which easily produced perfect dough in mere seconds. To keep the crust from becoming too soggy, we parbaked it before adding the filling. When it came to the filling, we found that a ratio of 5 eggs to 2 cups of half-and-half yielded a perfect creamy custard that was neither too rich nor too lean, and we could easily beat everything together in the processor. To enhance the sweet, buttery flavors of our quiche we added leeks that had been softened in butter. Here we again used the food processor to our advantage, swiftly slicing the fussy leeks into uniform half-moon pieces for quick and even cooking. We also added creamy goat cheese, which lent just the right amount of tang to balance the buttery leeks. A small amount of minced fresh chives provided the perfect herbal, oniony finish.

crust

3 tablespoons ice water, plus extra as needed

4 teaspoons sour cream

1¼ cups (6¼ ounces) all-purpose flour

1½ teaspoons sugar

½ teaspoon salt

8 tablespoons unsalted butter, cut into ¼-inch pieces and frozen for 10 to 15 minutes

filling

1 pound leeks, white and light green parts only, halved lengthwise

2 tablespoons unsalted butter

¾ teaspoon salt

4 ounces goat cheese, crumbled (1 cup)

5 large eggs

2 cups half-and-half

¼ teaspoon pepper

1 tablespoon minced fresh chives

1 for the crust Whisk ice water and sour cream together in bowl. Process flour, sugar, and salt in food processor until combined, about 3 seconds. Scatter frozen butter over top and pulse mixture until butter is size of large peas, about 10 pulses.

2 Pour half of sour cream mixture over flour mixture and pulse until incorporated, about 3 pulses. Repeat with remaining sour cream mixture. Pinch dough with your fingers; if dough feels dry and does not hold together, sprinkle 1 to 2 tablespoons more ice water over mixture and pulse until dough forms large clumps and no dry flour remains, 3 to 5 pulses.

3 Turn dough onto sheet of plastic wrap and flatten into 4-inch disk. Wrap tightly and refrigerate for 1 hour. Before rolling out dough, let it sit on counter to soften slightly,

about 10 minutes. (Dough can be refrigerated for up to 2 days or frozen for up to 1 month. If frozen, let dough thaw completely on counter before rolling it out.)

4 Roll dough between 2 large sheets of parchment paper into 12-inch circle. (If dough is soft and/or sticky, refrigerate until firm.) Remove parchment on top of dough round and flip into 9-inch pie plate; peel off second sheet of parchment. Lift dough and gently press into pie plate. Cover loosely with plastic and refrigerate until firm, about 30 minutes.

5 Trim all but ½ inch of dough overhanging edge of pie plate. Tuck dough underneath to form tidy, even edge that sits on lip of pie plate. Crimp dough evenly around edge of pie plate using fingers. Wrap dough-lined pie plate loosely in plastic and refrigerate until firm, about 15 minutes.

6 Adjust oven rack to middle position and heat oven to 400 degrees. Line chilled pie crust with double layer of aluminum foil, covering edges to prevent burning, and fill with pie weights or pennies. Bake until pie dough looks dry and is pale in color, 25 to 30 minutes. Transfer to rimmed baking sheet and remove weights and foil.

7 for the filling Reduce oven temperature to 350 degrees. Fit clean, dry food processor with slicing disk and process leeks until thinly sliced. Wash and drain leeks thoroughly. Melt butter in 10-inch nonstick skillet over medium-high heat. Add leeks and ½ teaspoon salt and cook until softened, about 6 minutes. Sprinkle leeks over bottom of warm pie shell and top with goat cheese.

8 Fit now-empty processor with chopping blade and process eggs, half-and-half, pepper, and remaining ¼ teaspoon salt until well combined, about 5 seconds. Place pie shell in oven and carefully pour in egg mixture until it reaches about ½ inch from top edge of crust (you may have extra egg mixture).

9 Bake quiche until top is lightly browned, center is set but soft, and knife inserted about 1 inch from edge comes out clean, 40 to 50 minutes. Let quiche cool for at least 1 hour or up to 3 hours. Sprinkle with chives and serve slightly warm or at room temperature.

ROASTED POBLANO AND BLACK BEAN ENCHILADAS

serves 4 to 6 **food processor size** 7 to 14 cups

why this recipe works Enchiladas are the definition of Mexican comfort food—a tortilla-wrapped savory filling, a flavorful sauce, and gooey melted cheese—but preparing them can require a fair amount of work. For a truly great, easy-prep version, we enlisted the food processor at multiple stages. We pureed canned tomatillos, onion, cilantro, garlic, lime juice, broth, and heavy cream for a rich, vibrant sauce. For the filling we pulsed together roasted poblano chiles and black beans, then added chili powder, cumin, and coriander to accent the Mexican flavors. We rolled the filling into warmed corn tortillas, topped them with our sauce, and finished the dish with a sprinkling of Monterey Jack cheese and a quick stint in the oven to bring everything together.

4 poblano chiles

8 ounces Monterey Jack cheese, chilled

2 (13-ounce) cans tomatillos, drained

1 onion, cut into 1-inch pieces

1 cup fresh cilantro leaves

⅓ cup vegetable broth

¼ cup heavy cream

3 tablespoons vegetable oil

5 garlic cloves, peeled and smashed

1 tablespoon lime juice

1 teaspoon sugar

Salt and pepper

1 (15-ounce) can black beans, rinsed

1 teaspoon chili powder

½ teaspoon ground coriander

½ teaspoon ground cumin

12 (6-inch) corn tortillas

1 Adjust oven rack 6 inches from broiler element and heat broiler. Place poblanos in aluminum foil–lined rimmed baking sheet and broil, turning as needed, until skins are charred, 15 to 20 minutes. Transfer poblanos to large bowl, cover with plastic wrap, and let steam for 5 minutes. Remove skins, stems, and seeds.

2 Adjust oven rack to middle position and heat oven to 400 degrees. Using food processor fitted with shredding disk, process Monterey Jack until shredded; set aside.

3 Fit now-empty processor with chopping blade and process tomatillos, onion, ½ cup cilantro, broth, cream, 1 tablespoon oil, 3 garlic cloves, lime juice, sugar, and 1 teaspoon salt until smooth, about 2 minutes, scraping down sides of bowl as needed. Season with salt and pepper to taste; set aside.

4 Pulse poblanos, half of beans, and remaining 2 garlic cloves in now-empty processor until coarsely chopped, about 8 pulses; transfer to large bowl. Stir in 1 cup Monterey Jack,

½ cup tomatillo sauce, chili powder, coriander, cumin, remaining whole beans, and remaining ½ cup cilantro until combined.

5 Spread ½ cup tomatillo sauce over bottom of 13 by 9-inch baking dish. Brush both sides of tortillas with remaining 2 tablespoons oil. Stack tortillas, wrap in damp dish towel, and place on plate; microwave until warm and pliable, about 1 minute. Working with 1 warm tortilla at a time, spread ¼ cup bean-cheese filling across center of tortilla. Roll tortilla tightly around filling and place, seam side down, in baking dish; arrange enchiladas in 2 columns across width of dish.

6 Pour remaining tomatillo sauce over top to cover completely and sprinkle remaining Monterey Jack down center of enchiladas. Cover dish tightly with greased aluminum foil and bake until enchiladas are heated through, about 25 minutes. Let cool for 5 minutes before serving.

VEGETABLE STIR-FRY WITH CRISPY TOFU

serves 4 to 6 **food processor size** 7 to 14 cups

why this recipe works Because it comes together very quickly over high heat, a great stir-fry depends on precisely prepared ingredients, which can be a challenge even for experienced cooks. We used the food processor to streamline the process and ensure that every element of the dish cooked up evenly. We started by slicing bok choy, shiitake mushrooms, carrots, and a red bell pepper in the processor. The neat, even vegetable slices quickly cooked up to a perfect crisp-tender texture. To make the dish a meal, we added tofu, which we pulsed in the processor before sautéeing to get crisp, golden-brown crumbles—a pleasant departure from cubes. A mixture of soy sauce, sherry, orange juice, garlic, ginger, and sesame oil plus a little brown sugar and cornstarch made a punchy glaze. For a final pop of crunch and freshness, we finished the dish with peanuts and scallions. You can use firm tofu instead of extra-firm for this recipe. Serve with rice.

14 ounces extra-firm tofu, cut into 2-inch pieces

10 ounces shiitake mushrooms, stemmed

2 carrots, peeled

1 red bell pepper, cored and quartered lengthwise

4 heads baby bok choy (4 ounces each), trimmed

3 tablespoons cornstarch

1 (2-inch) piece ginger, peeled and smashed

2 garlic cloves, peeled and smashed

3 tablespoons vegetable oil

¼ cup soy sauce

¼ cup dry sherry

¼ cup packed brown sugar

1 tablespoon toasted sesame oil

1 teaspoon grated orange zest plus ¼ cup juice

¼ cup dry-roasted peanuts, chopped

2 scallions, sliced thin on bias

1 Spread tofu on paper towel–lined baking sheet, let drain for 20 minutes, then gently press dry with paper towels.

2 Working in batches, use food processor fitted with slicing blade to process mushrooms, carrots, and pepper until thinly sliced; set aside. Process bok choy in now-empty processor until thinly sliced; set aside.

3 Fit again-empty processor with chopping blade and pulse tofu until coarsely chopped, about 5 pulses, stopping to redistribute tofu as needed. Line baking sheet with clean paper towels, spread tofu on sheet, and press gently with more paper towels to dry. Transfer tofu to bowl and toss with 2 tablespoons cornstarch.

4 Pulse ginger and garlic in again-empty processor until finely ground, about 8 pulses. Transfer ginger mixture to small bowl and stir in 1 teaspoon vegetable oil. Whisk soy sauce, sherry, sugar, sesame oil, orange zest and juice, and remaining 1 tablespoon cornstarch together in separate bowl.

5 Heat 2 tablespoons vegetable oil in 12-inch nonstick skillet over high heat until just smoking. Add tofu in single layer and cook, breaking up any clumps with wooden spoon, until well browned, 8 to 10 minutes; transfer to bowl.

6 Heat remaining 2 teaspoons vegetable oil in now-empty skillet over high heat until just smoking. Add mushrooms, carrots, and bell pepper and cook, stirring occasionally, until spotty brown, about 4 minutes. Push vegetables to sides of skillet. Add ginger mixture and cook, mashing mixture into skillet, until fragrant, 15 to 30 seconds. Stir ginger mixture into vegetables.

7 Add bok choy and cook until just wilted, about 1 minute. Whisk sauce to recombine, then add to skillet along with tofu. Cook, tossing constantly, until sauce is thickened, about 30 seconds. Off heat, sprinkle with peanuts and scallions. Serve.

MUSHROOM BOLOGNESE

serves 4 to 6   food processor size 7 to 14 cups

why this recipe works We wanted to create a vegetarian pasta sauce that mimicked the luxurious, long-cooked flavor and hearty texture of Bolognese. Traditional Bolognese sauce gets its rich flavor from a combination of several types of meat, so we turned to two types of mushrooms to replicate that complexity: Dried porcini delivered depth of flavor, and 2 pounds of fresh cremini gave the sauce a satisfying, substantial texture. To further round out the sauce's savory flavor, we added two umami-rich ingredients: soy sauce and tomato paste. To make prep easy, we used the food processor both to chop the cremini roughly and then to finely chop the onion and carrot. We also pulsed whole canned tomatoes in the food processor for the sauce, which allowed us to get just the right texture. To give the dish richness and depth, we added red wine, plus a little sugar for some balancing sweetness. A dash of heavy cream at the end rounded out the Bolognese and gave it a decadent silkiness.

2 pounds cremini mushrooms, trimmed and quartered

1 carrot, peeled and cut into 1-inch pieces

1 small onion, cut into 1-inch pieces

½ ounce dried porcini mushrooms, rinsed

3 garlic cloves, peeled and smashed

1 (28-ounce) can whole peeled tomatoes

3 tablespoons unsalted butter

2 tablespoons tomato paste

1 cup dry red wine

½ cup vegetable broth

1 tablespoon soy sauce

1 teaspoon sugar

Salt and pepper

3 tablespoons heavy cream

1 pound fettuccine or linguine

Grated Parmesan cheese

1 Working in batches, pulse cremini mushrooms in food processor until pieces are no larger than ½ inch, 5 to 7 pulses; transfer to large bowl. Pulse carrot, onion, porcini mushrooms, and garlic in now-empty processor until finely chopped, 5 to 7 pulses; transfer to bowl with mushrooms. Pulse tomatoes and their juice in now-empty processor until finely chopped, 6 to 8 pulses; set aside separately.

2 Melt butter in Dutch oven over medium heat. Add processed vegetables, cover, and cook, stirring occasionally, until they release their liquid, about 5 minutes. Uncover, increase heat to medium-high, and cook until liquid has evaporated and vegetables begin to brown, 12 to 15 minutes.

3 Stir in tomato paste and cook for 1 minute. Stir in wine and simmer until nearly evaporated, about 5 minutes. Stir in tomatoes, broth, soy sauce, sugar, ½ teaspoon salt, and ¼ teaspoon pepper. Bring to simmer and cook until sauce has thickened but is still moist, 8 to 10 minutes. Off heat, stir in cream.

4 Meanwhile, bring 4 quarts water to boil in large pot. Add pasta and 1 tablespoon salt and cook, stirring often, until al dente. Reserve ½ cup cooking water, then drain pasta and return it to pot. Add sauce and toss to combine. Season with salt and pepper to taste, and adjust consistency with reserved cooking water as needed. Serve with Parmesan.

PROVENÇAL VEGETABLE SOUP

serves 6   food processor size 7 to 14 cups

why this recipe works Provençal vegetable soup is a classic French summer soup with a delicate broth intensified by a dollop of *pistou*, the French equivalent of Italy's pesto. Bountiful amounts of chopped fresh summer vegetables are the key this flavorful soup. The slicing blade of the food processor made the prep work an approachable job even for a busy weeknight, and it produced thinly sliced results for a mixture of perfectly tender vegetables in every spoonful of soup. And with the processor already out, pureeing the pistou took just another minute. We added each vegetable to the soup at a specific time to ensure that they all came out perfectly done, starting with heartier leek, celery, and carrots and finishing with the more tender zucchini, haricots verts, and tomatoes. We added canned white beans (which were far more convenient than dried for this quick-cooking soup) and orecchiette pasta (for its easy-to-spoon shape) to round out this summery dish. We also simplified the traditional pistou by whirring together the basil, Parmesan, garlic, and oil in the food processor. If you cannot find haricots verts (thin green beans), substitute regular green beans and cook them for an extra minute or two. You can substitute small shells or ditalini for the orecchiette (the cooking times may vary slightly). Serve with crusty bread.

pistou

1 ounce Parmesan cheese, grated (½ cup)

½ cup fresh basil leaves

⅓ cup extra-virgin olive oil

1 garlic clove, peeled and smashed

soup

1 leek, white and light green parts only, halved lengthwise

8 ounces haricots verts, trimmed

1 small zucchini, halved lengthwise and seeded

2 plum tomatoes, cored and quartered lengthwise

1 celery rib

1 carrot, peeled

2 tablespoons extra-virgin olive oil

Salt and pepper

3 garlic cloves, minced

4 cups vegetable broth

3 cups water

½ cup orecchiette

1 (15-ounce) can cannellini or navy beans, rinsed

1 for the pistou Process all ingredients in food processor until smooth, about 8 seconds, scraping down sides of bowl as needed; set aside for serving.

2 for the soup Fit now-empty processor with slicing disk and process leek until thinly sliced. Wash and drain leek thoroughly; set aside. Working in batches, process haricots verts, zucchini, and tomatoes in again-empty processor until thinly sliced; set aside. Process celery and carrot in again-empty processor until thinly sliced.

3 Heat oil in Dutch oven over medium heat until shimmering. Add leek, celery, carrot, and ½ teaspoon salt and cook until vegetables are softened, 8 to 10 minutes. Stir in garlic and cook until fragrant, about 30 seconds. Stir in broth and water and bring to simmer.

4 Stir in pasta and cook until slightly softened, about 8 minutes. Stir in haricots verts, zucchini, tomatoes, and beans, return to simmer, and cook until pasta and vegetables are tender, 3 to 4 minutes. Season with salt and pepper to taste. Serve, topping individual portions with pistou.

BECOME YOUR OWN BUTCHER

Buying ground meat at the supermarket is kind of a crapshoot; unless your butcher grinds to order, there's no way to know what you're actually getting. The cut, fat content, and texture of store-ground meat can vary widely. But when you grind it yourself in a food processor, you control all the variables. That means you can achieve the perfect grind for beef, pork, poultry, and even fish and seafood. Your food processor can also help with thinly slicing meat, which can be a tricky task without a commercial meat slicer or a supersharp knife and an extremely steady hand. This opens up possibilities for all kinds of dishes in the home kitchen that are otherwise better left to the professionals.

FOOD PROCESSOR FINDINGS

Here are a few tricks we've discovered for grinding proteins in your food processor:

1 Partially freezing the meat before processing it ensures results that are chopped but not pulverized.

2 In dishes like our Ultimate Turkey Burgers (page 85) and Shrimp Burgers (page 86), we grind a portion of the main ingredient to a paste and use it to bind the rest of the dish, which is ground to a chunkier texture.

3 You can combine more than one cut of meat to engineer just the right mix of flavor and fat for each recipe.

4 To ensure clean, even cuts when slicing meat in the food processor, use a good amount of pressure to push the meat into the feed tube; don't be afraid to get a little heavy-handed!

5 Adding baking soda to our home-ground meat keeps it especially tender and moist during the cooking process. The soda raises the pH of the meat, which makes it more difficult for the proteins to bond.

6 You can use less panade (a bread and milk mixture used to add tenderness to ground meat dishes) when you grind your own meat because it will already be more tender than store-ground options.

GETTING THE PERFECT GRIND

Store-ground beef is often overprocessed to a pulp, so it cooks up heavy and dense no matter how much care you take. Processing home-ground meat just enough to get the perfect grind means it cooks up more tender. The exact size of the grind will depend on the type of meat and the type of dish; follow the visual cues given in each recipe.

underprocessed
(gristly and chunky)

overprocessed
(pasty and dense)

ground to perfection
(loose but tender)

JUICY PUB-STYLE BURGERS

serves 4 **food processor size** 7 to 14 cups

why this recipe works In our quest for the ideal hearty pub-style burger, we found that grinding our own meat was the best way to get big, beefy flavor and rich texture. We started by freezing meaty sirloin steak tips, which made them easier to grind to just the right coarse texture. A little melted butter improved juiciness. Lightly packing the patties gave the burgers enough structure without overworking the meat. Our biggest discovery was a two-step cooking process: The stovetop provided intense heat for searing, and then the oven's ambient heat allowed a gentle, even finish. A quick "special sauce" jazzed up the basic burger, and premium (but simple) additions made an appealing variation. Sirloin steak tips are often sold as flap meat. Do not overwork the meat or the burgers will be dense. For the best flavor, season the burgers aggressively just before cooking. To save time, prepare the other ingredients while the beef is in the freezer.

sauce

¾ cup mayonnaise

2 tablespoons soy sauce

1 tablespoon packed dark brown sugar

1 tablespoon Worcestershire sauce

1 tablespoon minced fresh chives

1 garlic clove, minced

¾ teaspoon pepper

burgers

2 pounds sirloin steak tips, trimmed and cut into ½-inch pieces

4 tablespoons unsalted butter, melted and cooled

Salt and pepper

1 teaspoon vegetable oil

4 large hamburger buns, toasted and buttered

1 for the sauce Whisk all ingredients together in bowl; refrigerate until ready to serve.

2 for the burgers Arrange beef in single layer in rimmed baking sheet and freeze until very firm and starting to harden around edges but still pliable, about 35 minutes.

3 Working in 4 batches, pulse beef in food processor until finely ground into 1/16-inch pieces, about 20 pulses, stopping to redistribute meat as needed; return to sheet. Spread ground beef over sheet, discarding any long strands of gristle and large chunks of fat.

4 Adjust oven rack to middle position and heat oven to 300 degrees. Drizzle beef with melted butter, sprinkle with 1 teaspoon pepper, and gently toss with fork to combine. Divide beef into 4 lightly packed balls, then gently flatten into ¾-inch-thick burgers. Refrigerate until ready to cook. (Burgers can be covered and refrigerated for up to 1 day.)

5 Season 1 side of burgers with salt and pepper. Using spatula, gently flip patties and season other side. Heat oil in 12-inch skillet over high heat until just smoking. Using spatula, transfer burgers to skillet and cook, without moving, for 2 minutes. Flip burgers and continue to cook for 2 minutes. Transfer to rimmed baking sheet and bake until burgers register 125 degrees (for medium-rare), 3 to 5 minutes. Transfer burgers to platter and let rest for 5 minutes before serving on buns with sauce.

JUICY PUB-STYLE BURGERS WITH PEPPERED BACON AND AGED CHEDDAR

Before cooking burgers, lay 6 slices of bacon in rimmed baking sheet. Sprinkle with 2 teaspoons coarsely ground pepper. Place second rimmed baking sheet on top of bacon. Bake in 375-degree oven until bacon is crisp, 15 to 20 minutes; transfer to paper towel–lined plate and let cool. Cut bacon in half crosswise. Before finishing burgers in oven, top with ¼ cup shredded aged cheddar cheese. Top with bacon before serving.

ULTIMATE TURKEY BURGERS

serves 6   food processor size 7 to 14 cups

why this recipe works To create juicy turkey burgers, we ditched store-bought ground turkey in favor of home-ground turkey thighs, which boast more fat and flavor. For just the right texture, we made a paste with a portion of ground turkey plus gelatin, soy sauce, and baking soda, which helped the burgers retain moisture. We also added chopped mushrooms for flavor and texture. A quick sear in a hot skillet followed by a stint in the oven gave us burgers that were anything but bland. A tangy sauce added welcome contrast to the mild meatiness of the turkey. If you are unable to find boneless, skinless turkey thighs, substitute one 2-pound bone-in thigh, skinned, boned, and trimmed. To ensure the best texture, don't let the burgers stand for more than an hour before cooking. To save time, prepare the other ingredients while the turkey is in the freezer.

sauce

¾ cup mayonnaise

4 teaspoons malt vinegar

½ teaspoon molasses

¼ teaspoon Worcestershire sauce

¼ teaspoon salt

¼ teaspoon pepper

burgers

1½ pounds boneless, skinless turkey thighs, trimmed and cut into ½-inch pieces

1 tablespoon unflavored gelatin

3 tablespoons chicken broth

6 ounces white mushrooms, trimmed

1 tablespoon soy sauce

Pinch baking soda

2 tablespoons plus 1 teaspoon vegetable oil

Salt and pepper

6 large hamburger buns, toasted

1 for the sauce Whisk all ingredients together in bowl; refrigerate until ready to serve.

2 for the burgers Arrange turkey in single layer in rimmed baking sheet and freeze until very firm and starting to harden around edges but still pliable, about 35 minutes.

3 Sprinkle gelatin over broth in small bowl and let sit until gelatin softens, about 5 minutes. Pulse mushrooms in food processor until coarsely chopped, about 7 pulses, stopping to redistribute mushrooms as needed; set aside.

4 Working in 3 batches, pulse turkey in now-empty processor until ground into ⅛-inch pieces, about 20 pulses, stopping to redistribute meat as needed; transfer to large bowl.

5 Return ½ cup (about 3 ounces) ground turkey to again-empty processor along with softened gelatin, soy sauce, and baking soda. Process until smooth, about 2 minutes, scraping down sides of bowl as needed. With processor running, slowly add 2 tablespoons oil until incorporated, about 10 seconds. Return mushrooms to processor with paste and pulse to combine, 3 to 5 pulses. Transfer mushroom mixture to bowl with turkey and knead with your hands until combined.

6 Adjust oven rack to middle position and heat oven to 300 degrees. With lightly greased hands, divide turkey mixture into 6 lightly packed balls, then gently flatten into ¾-inch-thick burgers. Refrigerate burgers until ready to cook. (Burgers can be covered and refrigerated for up to 1 day.)

7 Season 1 side of burgers with salt and pepper. Using spatula, gently flip burgers and season other side. Heat remaining 1 teaspoon oil in 12-inch nonstick skillet over high heat until just smoking. Using spatula, transfer burgers to skillet and cook, without moving, for 2 minutes. Flip burgers and continue to cook for 2 minutes. Transfer to rimmed baking sheet and bake until burgers register 160 degrees, 5 to 7 minutes. Transfer burgers to platter and let rest for 5 minutes before serving on buns with sauce.

SHRIMP BURGERS

serves 4   **food processor size** 7 to 14 cups

why this recipe works Home grinding isn't just for meat and poultry. To apply this technique to a different kind of burger, we turned to a specialty of southern coastal towns, the shrimp burger. Although the particulars may vary, a good shrimp burger should be first and foremost about the shrimp, so we kept things simple and let the sweetness of the seafood shine with an easy food processor method. We found that finely grinding a portion of the shrimp and some mayonnaise into a sticky paste effectively bound the rest of the processor-chopped shrimp without the need for eggs or a bready binder. We kept the seasonings light, using just salt, pepper, and cayenne and folding chopped scallions into the mix for a jolt of freshness. To mimic the crunchy exterior of deep-fried shrimp burgers, we ground panko to a fine powder before coating the burgers and sautéing them to a golden brown. We topped the burgers with a tangy five-ingredient tartar sauce.

tartar sauce

¾ cup mayonnaise

3 tablespoons sweet pickle relish

1½ teaspoons distilled white vinegar

½ teaspoon Worcestershire sauce

½ teaspoon pepper

burgers

1 cup panko bread crumbs

1½ pounds large shrimp (26 to 30 per pound), peeled, deveined, and tails removed

3 scallions, cut into 1-inch lengths

2 tablespoons mayonnaise

¼ teaspoon pepper

⅛ teaspoon salt

⅛ teaspoon cayenne pepper

3 tablespoons vegetable oil

4 large hamburger buns, toasted

4 leaves Bibb lettuce

1 for the tartar sauce Whisk all ingredients together in bowl; refrigerate until ready to serve.

2 for the burgers Pulse panko in food processor until finely ground, about 15 pulses; transfer to shallow dish. Place one-third of shrimp (about 1 cup), scallions, mayonnaise, pepper, salt, and cayenne in now-empty processor and pulse until shrimp are finely chopped, about 8 pulses. Add remaining shrimp and pulse until coarsely chopped, about 4 pulses, scraping down sides of bowl as needed.

3 With lightly greased hands, divide shrimp mixture into 4 lightly packed balls, then gently flatten into ¾-inch-thick burgers. Working with 1 burger at a time, dredge in panko, pressing lightly to adhere, and transfer to plate.

4 Heat oil in 12-inch nonstick skillet over medium heat until shimmering. Using spatula, transfer burgers to skillet and cook, without moving, until golden brown on first side, 3 to 5 minutes. Flip burgers and continue to cook until golden brown on second side and burgers register 140 to 145 degrees, 3 to 5 minutes. Transfer burgers to paper towel–lined plate and let drain, about 30 seconds per side. Spread tartar sauce on bun bottoms, then place patties and lettuce on top. Cover with bun tops. Serve.

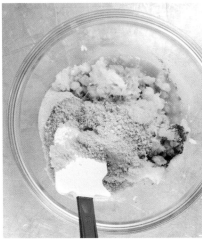

COD CAKES WITH GARLIC-BASIL AÏOLI

serves 4   food processor size 7 to 14 cups

why this recipe works Fish cakes are fast to make in the food processor, but many recipes add so much filler that the final product tastes more like bread crumbs than fish. For our version, we wanted to foreground the fresh cod, so we added just enough crunchy panko (plus a single egg) to hold the cakes together without affecting flavor. A light dredging in more panko created a crisp crust that turned golden once cooked. A quick garlicky aïoli, thrown together in the processor, dressed up the cod cakes, and we used a few tablespoons of it to add a touch more binding power as well as flavor to the cakes. We processed the cod (raw, not cooked) in two batches to avoid over-working the fish. Haddock and halibut are good substitutes for cod. It is important to avoid overprocessing the cod; it is OK to have some pieces that are larger than ¼ inch in step 2.

aïoli

½ cup mayonnaise

¼ cup fresh basil leaves

2 tablespoons lemon juice

1 garlic clove, peeled and smashed

Salt and pepper

cakes

1½ cups panko bread crumbs

1 pound skinless cod fillets, cut into 1-inch pieces

1 large egg, lightly beaten

½ teaspoon salt

¼ teaspoon pepper

¼ cup vegetable oil

1 for the aïoli Process mayonnaise, basil, lemon juice, and garlic in food processor until smooth and pale green, about 20 seconds, scraping down sides of bowl as needed. Transfer aïoli to bowl and season with salt and pepper to taste.

2 for the cakes Spread ¾ cup panko in shallow dish. Working in 2 batches, pulse cod in now-empty processor until chopped into ¼-inch pieces, about 2 pulses; transfer to large bowl. Gently fold in egg, 3 tablespoons aïoli, salt, pepper, and remaining ¾ cup panko until combined.

3 With lightly greased hands, divide cod mixture into 4 lightly packed balls, then gently flatten into 1-inch-thick patties. Working with 1 patty at a time, dredge in panko, pressing lightly to adhere, and transfer to plate.

4 Heat oil in 12-inch nonstick skillet over medium heat until shimmering. Using spatula, transfer patties to skillet and cook, without moving, until golden brown on first side, 3 to 5 minutes. Flip patties and continue to cook until golden brown on second side, 3 to 5 minutes. Transfer patties to paper towel–lined plate and let drain, about 30 seconds per side. Serve with remaining aïoli.

THAI PORK LETTUCE WRAPS

serves 4 **food processor size** 7 to 14 cups

why this recipe works We wanted to replicate the classic light, pungent Thai salad of boldly flavored minced pork (or sometimes beef or chicken) known as *larb*. Instead of working with preground pork from the supermarket, which we found to have inconsistent texture and fat content, we chopped pork tenderloin in the food processor and then marinated it in a little fish sauce so it would retain moisture during cooking. To balance our recipe's blend of tart (lime juice), salty (fish sauce), and hot (pepper flakes) flavors, we added a little sugar. Toasted rice powder contributed a nutty flavor and texture to the pork. For the aromatic components, the pungency of sliced shallots and the bright flavor of chopped mint and cilantro yielded a very flavorful salad without a trip to a specialty store. We prefer natural pork in this recipe. If using enhanced pork, skip the marinating in step 3 and reduce the amount of fish sauce to 2 tablespoons, adding it all in step 6. Don't skip toasting the rice; it's integral to the texture and flavor of the dish. Any style of white rice can be used. You can use store-bought toasted rice powder (*kao kua*), which can be found in Asian markets, if you don't want to make your own. This dish can be served with sticky rice and steamed vegetables as an entrée. To save time, prepare the other ingredients while the pork is in the freezer.

1 (1-pound) pork tenderloin, trimmed and cut into 1-inch pieces

2 shallots, peeled

2½ tablespoons fish sauce

1 tablespoon white rice

¼ cup chicken broth

3 tablespoons chopped fresh mint

3 tablespoons chopped fresh cilantro

3 tablespoons lime juice (2 limes)

2 teaspoons sugar

¼ teaspoon red pepper flakes

1 head Bibb lettuce (8 ounces), leaves separated and left whole

1 Arrange pork in single layer in rimmed baking sheet and freeze until firm and starting to harden around edges but still pliable, 15 to 20 minutes.

2 Using food processor fitted with slicing disk, process shallots until thinly sliced; set aside.

3 Fit now-empty processor with chopping blade. Working in 2 batches, pulse pork in processor until coarsely chopped, about 5 pulses; transfer to bowl. Toss pork with 1 tablespoon fish sauce, cover, and refrigerate for 15 minutes.

4 Toast rice in 12-inch nonstick skillet over medium-high heat, stirring constantly, until deep golden brown, about 5 minutes. Transfer rice to small bowl, let cool for 5 minutes,

then grind into fine meal using spice grinder (10 to 30 seconds) or mortar and pestle (you should have about 1 tablespoon rice powder).

5 Bring broth to simmer in now-empty skillet over medium-high heat. Add pork and cook, stirring frequently, until pork is about half-pink, about 2 minutes. Sprinkle 1 teaspoon rice powder into skillet and cook, stirring constantly, until pork is no longer pink, about 2 minutes.

6 Transfer pork to large bowl and let cool for 10 minutes. Stir in shallots, mint, cilantro, lime juice, sugar, pepper flakes, remaining 1½ tablespoons fish sauce, and remaining rice powder and toss to combine. Serve in lettuce leaves.

STEAK AND CHEESE SANDWICHES

serves 4 food processor size 7 to 14 cups

why this recipe works Making steak and cheese sandwiches reminiscent of the famously rich Philadelphia cheesesteaks required finding a simple and economical way to mimic the thinly shaved slivers of steak usually obtained with a meat slicer. We found that when mostly frozen, skirt steak's thin profile and open-grained texture made for easy slicing, and its flavor was close to that of the traditional rib eye but without the sticker shock. The food processor gave us clean, consistently thin slices with almost no effort. We also used the food processor to slice up mushrooms and an onion for a heartier filling. To best approximate the wide griddle typically used in Philadelphia, we cooked the meat in two batches, letting any excess moisture drain off before giving it a final sear. Finally, to bind it all together, we let American cheese melt into the meat, along with a bit of grated Parmesan to boost its flavor. If skirt steak is unavailable, sirloin steak tips (also called flap meat) make an acceptable substitute. To save time, prepare the other ingredients while the beef is in the freezer. These sandwiches can be topped with pickled hot peppers, sweet relish, or hot sauce.

2 pounds skirt steak, trimmed and sliced with grain into 3-inch-wide strips

1 onion, quartered through root end

12 ounces cremini mushrooms, trimmed

3 tablespoons vegetable oil

Salt and pepper

¼ cup grated Parmesan cheese

8 ounces sliced American cheese

4 (8-inch) Italian sub rolls, split lengthwise and toasted

1 Arrange beef in single layer in rimmed baking sheet and freeze until very firm and starting to harden around edges but still pliable, 45 to 60 minutes.

2 Working in batches, use food processor fitted with slicing disk to process onion and mushrooms until thinly sliced; set aside. Process beef against grain in now-empty processor until thinly sliced.

3 Heat 1 tablespoon oil in 12-inch nonstick skillet over medium-high heat until shimmering. Add onion and mushrooms and cook until softened and lightly browned, about 10 minutes; transfer to colander set over bowl.

4 Heat 1 tablespoon oil in now-empty skillet over high heat until just smoking. Add half of beef in even layer and cook, without stirring, until well browned on one side, about 5 minutes. Stir and continue to cook until beef is no longer pink, about 2 minutes; transfer to colander with onion and mushrooms. Repeat with remaining 1 tablespoon oil and remaining beef.

5 Drain onion mixture and beef and return to again-empty skillet with ½ teaspoon salt and ⅛ teaspoon pepper. Cook over medium heat, stirring occasionally, until heated through, about 2 minutes. Reduce heat to low. Sprinkle beef mixture with Parmesan and shingle with American cheese. Allow cheeses to melt, about 2 minutes. Using heatproof spatula or wooden spoon, fold melted cheese into meat mixture until thoroughly combined. Serve in rolls.

HOMEMADE ITALIAN-STYLE SAUSAGES AND PEPPERS

serves 4 to 6   **food processor size** 7 to 14 cups

why this recipe works Store-bought Italian sausages can vary widely in fat, flavor, and greasiness. For a great sausage with balanced flavor and no added preservatives, we decided to make our own in the food processor. To keep this homemade sausage approachable, we wanted to avoid fussing with casings and keep the ingredient list simple. Grinding our own meat gave us control over the fat content. We started with carefully trimmed pork butt and then added fat back into the mixture by incorporating salt pork. After experimenting, we found that a 70:30 ratio of meat to fat made for the juiciest, most flavorful sausages. Grinding the salt pork to a paste and then mixing it with the meat gave us the most consistent texture. We also treated the meat with baking soda, a trick we learned to help keep ground meat moist and tender, and added garlic, oregano, fennel, and pepper flakes, which are traditional in Italian sausages. We shaped the mixture into rough sausage links, which was easy even without casings, and our shaped sausages fit perfectly in traditional buns. After browning the sausages on all sides, we finished the dish by simmering the sausages, along with peppers and onions, in a simple tomato sauce to build complex, robust flavor. A shot of balsamic vinegar, added at the end, provided a welcome counterpoint to the sweetness of the peppers. Pork butt roast is often labeled "Boston butt" in the supermarket. Make sure to rinse the salt pork well; otherwise the sausages will be too salty. You should have about 2 pounds of meat once the pork butt has been trimmed. To save time, prepare the other ingredients while the pork is in the freezer. Serve these sausages as is or in toasted buns.

12 ounces salt pork, rind removed, cut into ½-inch pieces

3 pounds boneless pork butt roast, pulled apart at seams, trimmed, and cut into ½-inch pieces

2 green or red bell peppers, cored and quartered lengthwise

2 onions, quartered through root end

¾ teaspoon baking soda

3 garlic cloves, peeled and smashed

2 teaspoons dried oregano

1½ teaspoons fennel seeds, cracked

Salt and pepper

¼ teaspoon red pepper flakes

1 tablespoon vegetable oil

¼ cup tomato paste

½ cup chicken broth

1 tablespoon balsamic vinegar

1 Rinse salt pork and pat dry with paper towels. Arrange salt pork and pork butt separately in single layer in rimmed baking sheet. Freeze until very firm and starting to harden around edges but still pliable, about 45 minutes.

2 Working in batches, use food processor fitted with slicing disk to process bell peppers and onions until thinly sliced; set aside.

3 Fit now-empty processor with chopping blade. Sprinkle baking soda evenly over pork butt. Working in 6 batches, pulse pork butt in processor until ground into ⅛-inch pieces, about 10 pulses, stopping to redistribute meat as needed; transfer to large bowl.

4 Pulse salt pork, garlic, 1½ teaspoons oregano, fennel seeds, ½ teaspoon pepper, and pepper flakes in again-empty processor to smooth paste, about 30 seconds, scraping down sides of bowl as needed. Transfer salt pork mixture to bowl with pork butt and knead with your hands until well combined.

5 Divide sausage mixture into 12 lightly packed balls, then gently shape into 5 by 1-inch cylinders. Refrigerate sausages until ready to cook. (Sausages can be covered and refrigerated for up to 1 day.)

6 Heat oil in 12-inch nonstick skillet over medium heat until shimmering. Brown half of sausages on all sides, about 10 minutes; transfer to plate. Repeat with remaining sausages.

7 Pour off all but 1 tablespoon fat from skillet, add tomato paste and remaining ½ teaspoon oregano, and cook until fragrant, about 30 seconds. Stir in bell peppers, onions, and broth.

8 Nestle sausages into vegetable mixture along with any accumulated juices and bring to simmer. Reduce heat to low, cover, and simmer until sausages and vegetables are tender, about 15 minutes. Stir in vinegar and season with salt and pepper to taste. Serve.

MEATBALLS AND MARINARA

makes 24 meatballs and about 14 cups sauce, enough for 2 pounds of pasta   food processor size 7 to 14 cups

why this recipe works Comfort food doesn't have to be boring. We saw just how good a simple burger could be if we ground our own meat, so it seemed obvious to apply that lesson to the challenge of making the ultimate meatball, with all the rich flavor and tender texture that you can get only when you have control over the cuts of meat. We tried chuck steak, steak tips alone, steak tips with country-style ribs, and steak tips with short ribs. By far, we preferred the meaty, unctuous flavor of short ribs in our meatballs. We tinkered with the mixture, finally settling on a 2:1 ratio of steak tips to short ribs. To further keep the ground meat moist and tender, we treated it with a small amount of baking soda. The alkali baking soda helped the meat hold onto moisture, so it didn't shed too much liquid during cooking. We found that with the short ribs and the baking soda, we could cut back on the bread-crumbs-and-milk panade that we usually add to meatballs to keep them moist, which meant even meatier meatballs in our home-ground version. For an easier method than pan frying, we turned to the oven and roasted our big batch of meatballs all at once at a high temperature, which ensured that they developed a nice browned crust. We then finished the meatballs with a simmer in a quick homemade tomato sauce. Sirloin steak tips are often sold as flap meat. We prefer using a mix of steak tips and short ribs in this recipe; however, you can use all steak tips, if desired. To save time, prepare the other ingredients while the beef is in the freezer.

meatballs

2 pounds sirloin steak tips, trimmed and cut into ½-inch pieces

1 pound boneless beef short ribs, trimmed and cut into ½-inch pieces

1 teaspoon baking soda

2 slices hearty white sandwich bread, torn into 1-inch pieces

2 large eggs

2 ounces Parmesan cheese, grated (1 cup)

½ cup fresh parsley leaves

¼ cup milk

2 teaspoons salt

sauce

3 onions, cut into 1-inch pieces

8 garlic cloves, peeled and smashed

1 tablespoon dried oregano

¾ teaspoon red pepper flakes

¼ cup extra-virgin olive oil

1 (6-ounce) can tomato paste

1 cup dry red wine

1 cup water

4 (28-ounce) cans crushed tomatoes

1 teaspoon salt

¼ cup minced fresh basil

1 for the meatballs Toss steak tips and short ribs together in rimmed baking sheet and spread into single layer. Freeze until very firm and starting to harden around edges but still pliable, about 45 minutes.

2 for the sauce Meanwhile, pulse onions, garlic, oregano, and pepper flakes in food processor until finely chopped, about 10 pulses. Heat oil in Dutch oven over medium heat until

shimmering. Add onion mixture and cook until softened and lightly browned, 10 to 15 minutes. Set aside half of onion mixture for meatballs.

3 Stir tomato paste into remaining onion mixture and cook over medium heat until fragrant, about 1 minute. Stir in wine, scraping up any browned bits, and cook until slightly

thickened, about 2 minutes. Stir in water, tomatoes, and salt. Bring to simmer and cook until sauce is no longer watery, 45 to 60 minutes.

4 Meanwhile, adjust oven rack to upper-middle position and heat oven to 475 degrees. Set wire rack in aluminum foil–lined rimmed baking sheet and spray with vegetable oil spray. Sprinkle baking soda evenly over beef. Working in 6 batches, pulse beef in now-empty food processor until finely ground into $\frac{1}{16}$-inch pieces, about 20 pulses, stopping to redistribute meat as needed; transfer to large bowl.

5 Process bread, eggs, Parmesan, parsley, milk, salt, and remaining onion mixture in again-empty processor until smooth, about 20 seconds, scraping down sides of bowl as needed. Transfer bread mixture to bowl with beef and knead with your hands until well combined.

6 Pinch off and roll beef mixture into 2-inch meatballs (you should have 24 meatballs), place on prepared rack, and bake until well browned, about 20 minutes. Transfer meatballs to pot with sauce and simmer for 15 minutes. Stir in basil and season with salt and pepper to taste. Serve. (Meatballs and marinara can be refrigerated for up to 3 days or frozen for up to 1 month.)

HOME-GROUND BEEF CHILI

serves 8 to 10   **food processor size** 7 to 14 cups

why this recipe works Once we'd developed a foolproof method for using the food processor as a meat grinder, we turned to one of our favorite ground beef recipes: thick, spicy, ultrabeefy chili. Making our own ground beef from meaty chuck roast helped give the chili all the hearty texture and juiciness of a traditional chili made with chunks of beef. And we didn't stop there—we also used the processor to make our own chili powder out of toasted dried ancho chiles, chipotle chile in adobo, and paprika, along with a blend of herbs and spices, and ground tortilla chips for added thickness and toasty corn flavor. To keep the meat moist and tender, we treated it with baking soda, which kept the meat from shedding too much liquid during cooking. To further highlight the beef, we kept filler to a minimum, using only small amounts of pureed whole canned tomatoes and pinto beans. We also made sure to stir in any fat that collected on the top of the chili before serving since it contained much of the flavor from the fat-soluble spices in the chili powder. To save time, prepare the other ingredients while the beef is in the freezer. This chili is intensely flavored and should be served with tortilla chips and/or plenty of steamed white rice as well as your favorite toppings.

2½ pounds boneless beef chuck-eye roast, pulled apart at seams, trimmed, and cut into ½-inch pieces

6 dried ancho chiles, stemmed, seeded, and torn into 1-inch pieces (1½ cups)

¾ teaspoon baking soda

1 ounce tortilla chips, crushed (¼ cup)

2 tablespoons ground cumin

1 tablespoon paprika

1 tablespoon garlic powder

1 tablespoon ground coriander

2 teaspoons dried oregano

½ teaspoon dried thyme

Salt and pepper

1 onion, cut into 1-inch pieces

3 garlic cloves, peeled and smashed

1 (14.5-ounce) can whole peeled tomatoes

1 tablespoon vegetable oil

1 teaspoon minced canned chipotle chile in adobo sauce

2 cups water

1 (15-ounce) can pinto beans

2 teaspoons sugar

2 tablespoons cider vinegar

1 Arrange beef in single layer in rimmed baking sheet and freeze until very firm and starting to harden around edges but still pliable, about 35 minutes.

2 Meanwhile, place anchos in Dutch oven set over medium-high heat and toast, stirring frequently, until fragrant, 4 to 6 minutes, reducing heat if anchos begin to smoke; set aside.

3 Sprinkle baking soda evenly over meat. Working in 6 batches, pulse beef in food processor until finely ground into 1⁄16-inch pieces, about 20 pulses, stopping to redistribute meat as needed; transfer to bowl.

4 Add anchos, tortilla chips, cumin, paprika, garlic powder, coriander, oregano, thyme, 1½ teaspoons salt, and 2 teaspoons pepper to now-empty processor and process until finely ground, about 2 minutes; set aside.

5 Pulse onion and garlic in again-empty processor until finely chopped, about 8 pulses; set aside. Process tomatoes and their juice in again-empty processor until smooth, about 30 seconds.

6 Adjust oven rack to lower-middle position and heat oven to 275 degrees. Heat oil in now-empty pot over medium-high heat until shimmering. Add onion mixture and cook, stirring occasionally, until softened, about 5 minutes. Add beef and cook, breaking up meat with wooden spoon, until browned and fond begins to form on pot bottom, 10 to 12 minutes. Add ancho mixture and chipotle and cook, stirring frequently, until fragrant, 1 to 2 minutes.

7 Stir in water, beans and their liquid, sugar, and tomatoes. Bring to boil, scraping bottom of pot to loosen any browned bits. Cover, transfer pot to oven, and cook until meat is tender and chili is slightly thickened, 1½ to 2 hours, stirring occasionally to prevent sticking.

8 Remove chili from oven and let sit, uncovered, for 10 minutes. Stir in any fat that has risen to top of chili, then add vinegar and season with salt to taste. Serve.

MEATIER MEATLOAF

serves 6 to 8 **food processor size** 7 to 14 cups

why this recipe works For the ultimate version of this family favorite, we went all out to amp up the flavor and juiciness. Meatloaf mix is usually a mysterious combination of leftover bits of beef, pork, and veal, preground at the store. Grinding our own meat put us in control and gave us all kinds of options in terms of which types of meat and cuts we could use. In the end, we opted to combine rich, flavorful steak tips with country-style pork ribs, which had mild, sweet notes that gave us a nicely balanced mixture. We also added a little gelatin, which can absorb up to 10 times its weight in water. This helped the loaf stay juicy and allowed us to leave out the traditional veal, which is usually included because it is gelatin rich (but which has a relatively meek flavor). To help boost the moisture even more, we included umami-rich mushrooms. Browning the mushrooms with tomato paste and mixing in chicken broth and soy sauce contributed additional savory notes. With all these moisture-enhancing tricks, we found we could cut back on panade, and with less bread-crumb filler, we got even better meaty flavor. Cooking the meatloaf free-form on a rack maximized browning and prevented the loaf from stewing or steaming in the pan. To save time, prepare the other ingredients while the beef is in the freezer.

meatloaf

1 pound boneless country-style pork ribs, trimmed and cut into ½-inch pieces

1 pound sirloin steak tips, trimmed and cut into ½-inch pieces

½ cup chicken broth

2 large eggs

2 tablespoons soy sauce

1 tablespoon unflavored gelatin

6 tablespoons unsalted butter

6 ounces white mushrooms, trimmed and quartered

1 onion, cut into 1-inch pieces

1 tablespoon tomato paste

2 garlic cloves, peeled and smashed

1 slice hearty white sandwich bread, torn into 1-inch pieces

⅓ cup fresh parsley leaves

2 teaspoons Dijon mustard

2 teaspoons minced fresh thyme or ½ teaspoon dried

Salt and pepper

¾ teaspoon baking soda

glaze

½ cup ketchup

¼ cup cider vinegar

3 tablespoons packed brown sugar

1 teaspoon hot sauce

½ teaspoon ground coriander

1 for the meatloaf Toss pork and beef together in rimmed baking sheet and spread into even layer. Freeze until very firm and starting to harden around edges but still pliable, about 35 minutes.

2 Meanwhile, adjust oven rack to middle position and heat oven to 350 degrees. Fold heavy-duty aluminum foil to form 10 by 6-inch rectangle. Center foil on wire rack set in foil-lined rimmed baking sheet. Poke holes in foil with skewer, about ½ inch apart. Spray foil with vegetable oil spray; set aside.

3 Whisk broth, eggs, and soy sauce together in bowl. Sprinkle gelatin over egg mixture and let sit until gelatin softens, about 5 minutes.

4 Melt butter in 12-inch nonstick skillet over medium heat. Add mushrooms and onion and cook until softened and lightly browned, 10 to 12 minutes. Add tomato paste and garlic and cook until fragrant, about 1 minute. Transfer mushroom mixture to bowl and let cool slightly.

5 Pulse bread in food processor until finely ground, 5 to 10 pulses. Add egg mixture, mushroom mixture, parsley, mustard, thyme, 1 teaspoon salt, and ¾ teaspoon pepper and pulse until mushrooms are finely ground, about 10 pulses, scraping down sides of bowl as needed; transfer to large bowl.

6 Sprinkle baking soda evenly over meat. Working in 6 batches, pulse meat in now-empty food processor until finely ground into 1/16-inch pieces, about 20 pulses, stopping to redistribute meat as needed; transfer to bowl with bread mixture.

7 Knead meat and bread mixture with your hands until combined. Transfer to prepared foil rectangle and shape into 9 by 5-inch loaf using wet hands. Bake meatloaf until it registers 155 to 160 degrees, about 1 hour. Remove from oven and turn on broiler.

8 for the glaze While meatloaf cooks, bring all ingredients to simmer in small saucepan over medium heat. Cook, stirring occasionally, until thick and syrupy, about 5 minutes.

9 Spread half of glaze evenly over meatloaf, place under broiler, and cook until glaze bubbles and begins to brown at edges, about 2 minutes. Remove meatloaf from oven and spread evenly with remaining glaze. Return to broiler and cook until glaze is again bubbling and beginning to brown, about 2 minutes. Let cool for 20 minutes before slicing.

KNEAD DOUGH IN NO TIME AT ALL

For bubbly, airy loaves of bread and perfect chewy crusts, you need to build up gluten. Gluten is a strong network of cross-linked proteins that traps gas bubbles and stretches as the dough bakes. Gluten is developed by kneading, but creating enough gluten in a wet mixture like pizza dough can take up to 20 minutes if you're kneading by hand. You could use a stand mixer, but by far the fastest, easiest way to knead almost any dough is in the food processor. The rapid action of a food processor's blade can turn dough elastic in just minutes with almost no effort. The food processor also helps ensure that the dry and wet ingredients are evenly incorporated and helps avoid unmixed pockets of flour for the most effortless doughs you'll ever make.

FOOD PROCESSOR FINDINGS

Here are a few tricks we've discovered for making and kneading doughs in your food processor:

1 Many food processors come with dull plastic "dough blades," but we found they are not the best tool for the job. They tend to drag the dough or leave it stuck to the sides of the bowl, out of reach of their stubby blades. The regular metal blade is far better at forming and kneading the dough quickly and effectively.

2 The forceful action of a food processor creates friction, pumping a lot of heat into dough. To counteract this effect, which can kill yeast and stunt both rise and flavor, it's important to use chilled or iced liquids when you make dough in a food processor.

3 Don't overknead, especially if the dough is enriched with butter; the heat from the processor can soften the butter too much, which affects the texture of the bread.

4 Add the liquid ingredients to the dry ingredients while the processor is running to make sure they get mixed together quickly and evenly. If you pour the liquid on top of the dry ingredients and then turn on the processor, the liquid can overflow the workbowl and make a mess.

KNEAD TO KNOW

When properly kneaded, dough should have a smooth, almost shiny appearance. If you pull the dough, it should feel very stretchy and quickly spring back into place. The photos below show what underkneaded, properly kneaded, and overkneaded doughs look like in the food processor.

underkneaded (breaks when pulled)

properly kneaded (fully elastic)

overkneaded (tough and dense)

FLUFFY DINNER ROLLS

makes 15 rolls   food processor size 14 cups

why this recipe works We wanted a rich, fluffy dinner roll with minimal fuss. To keep things simple, we turned to the food processor: Its quick-moving blade combined the dough in a matter of seconds, and its powerful motor did the kneading for us. For the dough, we used a combination of butter and shortening for the best flavor and a soft crumb, and we further enriched the dough with whole milk and an egg. Honey added a hint of sweetness. We lined the baking dish with a foil sling before adding the shaped dough so it was easy to get the baked rolls out of the pan. Finally, an egg wash brushed on the dough before baking gave the rolls a deep golden-brown color. This dough can be refrigerated overnight after you shape it into rolls. It is important to use chilled milk in the dough to prevent it from overheating in the food processor.

⅓ cup honey

4 tablespoons vegetable shortening, melted

3 tablespoons unsalted butter, melted

1 large egg

5 cups (25 ounces) all-purpose flour

2¼ teaspoons instant or rapid-rise yeast

2 teaspoons salt

1½ cups whole milk, chilled

1 large egg, lightly beaten with 1 tablespoon water and pinch salt

1 Whisk honey, shortening, butter, and egg together in 4-cup liquid measuring cup until honey has dissolved. Pulse flour, yeast, and salt in food processor until combined, about 5 pulses. With processor running, add milk, then honey mixture, and process until dough forms rough, elastic ball that begins to clear sides of bowl, 30 seconds to 1 minute.

2 Transfer dough to lightly floured counter. Using your lightly floured hands, knead dough to form smooth, round ball, about 30 seconds. Place dough seam side down in lightly greased large bowl or container, cover tightly with plastic wrap, and let rise until doubled in size, 1½ to 2 hours.

3 Make foil sling for 13 by 9-inch baking dish by folding 2 long sheets of aluminum foil; first sheet should be 13 inches wide and second sheet should be 9 inches wide. Lay sheets of foil in dish perpendicular to each other, with extra foil hanging over edges of dish. Push foil into corners and up sides of dish, smoothing foil flush to dish, then spray foil with vegetable oil spray.

4 Press down on dough to deflate. Transfer dough to clean counter and stretch into even 15-inch log. Cut log into 15 equal pieces (about 3 ounces each) and cover loosely with greased plastic.

5 Working with 1 piece of dough at a time (keep remaining pieces covered), form into rough ball by stretching dough around your thumbs and pinching edges together so the top is smooth. Place ball seam side down on clean counter and, using your cupped hand, drag in small circles until dough feels taut and round.

6 Arrange dough balls seam side down into 5 rows of 3 in prepared dish, cover loosely with greased plastic, and let rise until nearly doubled in size and dough springs back minimally when poked gently with your knuckle, 1 to 1½ hours. (Unrisen rolls can be refrigerated for up to 16 hours; let rolls sit at room temperature for 1 hour before baking.)

7 Adjust oven rack to lower-middle position and heat oven to 350 degrees. Gently brush rolls with egg mixture and bake until golden brown, 25 to 30 minutes, rotating dish halfway through baking. Let rolls cool in dish for 15 minutes. Using foil sling, transfer rolls to wire rack. Serve warm or at room temperature.

GARLIC KNOTS

makes 12 knots **food processor size** 11 to 14 cups

why this recipe works Typically made from leftover pizza dough, buttery, supremely garlicky garlic knots are a pizzeria classic. But when we tried to engineer them from scratch, the pizza dough recipes we tried made knots that were too dry or too hard. We wanted something fluffier than pizza crust but chewier than dinner rolls. Classic recipes call for kneading the dough exhaustively in a stand mixer to achieve that perfect chew, but the food processor can do the same work in a fraction of the time. Using all-purpose flour instead of higher-protein bread flour gave us a softer, fluffier interior. To give our knots potent flavor, we first tried garlic powder, but that tasted artificial, and raw garlic was too harsh. We settled on sautéing nine cloves of garlic—minced in seconds in the food processor—in butter, some of which we then added to the dough, along with the reserved toasty garlic solids. We brushed the knots with more garlic butter during baking and again just after taking them out of the oven for a version of this snack that satisfied our major garlic cravings. It is important to use ice water in the dough to prevent it from overheating in the food processor.

9 garlic cloves, peeled

6 tablespoons unsalted butter

1 teaspoon water, plus ¾ cup ice water

2 cups (10 ounces) all-purpose flour

1½ teaspoons instant or rapid-rise yeast

1 teaspoon salt

Coarse sea salt

1 Pulse garlic in food processor until finely chopped, about 10 pulses, scraping down sides of bowl as needed. Cook garlic, 1 tablespoon butter, and 1 teaspoon water in 8-inch skillet over low heat, stirring occasionally, until garlic is straw-colored, 8 to 10 minutes. Stir in remaining 5 tablespoons butter until melted. Strain into bowl; reserve garlic solids.

2 Pulse flour, yeast, and salt in now-empty processor until combined, about 5 pulses. With processor running, add ice water, then 1 tablespoon garlic butter and garlic solids, and process until dough forms rough, elastic ball that begins to clear sides of bowl, 30 seconds to 1 minute.

3 Transfer dough to lightly floured counter. Using your lightly floured hands, knead dough to form smooth, round ball, about 30 seconds. Place dough seam side down in lightly greased large bowl or container, cover tightly with plastic wrap, and let rise until doubled in size, 1 to 1½ hours.

4 Line rimmed baking sheet with parchment paper. Press down on dough to deflate. Transfer dough to clean counter. Press and stretch dough into 12 by 6-inch rectangle, with long side parallel to counter edge.

5 Using pizza cutter or chef's knife, cut dough vertically into twelve 6 by 1-inch strips; cover loosely with greased plastic. Working with 1 piece of dough at a time (keep remaining pieces covered), stretch and roll into 14-inch rope.

6 Shape rope into U with 2-inch-wide bottom curve. Tie ends into single overhand knot, with 1½-inch open loop at bottom. Wrap 1 tail over loop and press through opening from top. Wrap other tail under loop and through opening from bottom. Tuck one tail into center of loop and pull other tail up through center of loop.

7 Arrange knots on prepared sheet, spaced about 1 inch apart. Cover loosely with greased plastic and let rise until nearly doubled in size and dough springs back minimally when poked gently with your knuckle, 1 to 1½ hours. (Unrisen garlic knots can be refrigerated for up to 16 hours; let garlic knots sit at room temperature for 1 hour before baking.)

8 Adjust oven rack to middle position and heat oven to 500 degrees. Bake knots until set, about 5 minutes. Brush with 2 tablespoons garlic butter, rotate sheet, and bake until knots are golden brown, about 5 minutes. Transfer knots to wire rack. Brush with remaining garlic butter, sprinkle with sea salt, and let cool for 15 minutes. Serve warm.

AMERICAN SANDWICH BREAD

makes 1 loaf   **food processor size** 11 to 14 cups

why this recipe works The quintessential American sandwich loaf—tall and domed, with a fine, snowy-white crumb and a light brown crust—is a supermarket staple. In developing our sandwich loaf, we wanted a recipe that wasn't just better than bouncy plastic-wrapped bread, but the best—a worthy base for sandwiches. This proved simple to achieve with a food processor, which created a dough that required only a tiny bit of hand kneading. To get the bread's soft crumb, we included a fair amount of fat; we used whole milk as the majority of the liquid and then enriched the dough further with 2 tablespoons of melted butter. A couple of spoonfuls of honey gave the bread the faint sweetness we were looking for in this type of loaf. However, because our dough contained milk, butter, and honey, the crust was prone to browning before the inside was done. We tested oven temperatures and found that 350 degrees gave us the soft crust we wanted and avoided a doughy interior. The test kitchen's preferred loaf pan measures 8½ by 4½ inches; if you use a 9 by 5-inch loaf pan, increase the shaped rising time by 20 to 30 minutes and start checking for doneness 10 minutes earlier than advised in the recipe. It is important to use chilled milk and ice water in the dough to prevent it from overheating in the food processor.

2 tablespoons unsalted butter, melted

2 tablespoons honey

¾ cup whole milk, chilled

⅓ cup ice water

2½ cups (13¾ ounces) bread flour

2 teaspoons instant or rapid-rise yeast

1½ teaspoons salt

1 Whisk butter and honey together in 4-cup liquid measuring cup until honey has dissolved. Whisk in milk and ice water until combined.

2 Pulse flour, yeast, and salt in food processor until combined, about 5 pulses. With processor running, add milk mixture and process until dough forms rough, elastic ball that begins to clear sides of bowl, 30 seconds to 1 minute.

3 Transfer dough to lightly floured counter. Using your lightly floured hands, knead dough to form smooth, round ball, about 30 seconds. Place dough seam side down in lightly greased large bowl or container, cover tightly with plastic wrap, and let rise until doubled in size, 1½ to 2 hours.

4 Grease 8½ by 4½-inch loaf pan. Press down gently on dough to deflate. Turn dough out onto lightly floured counter (side of dough that was against bowl should now be facing up). Press and stretch dough into 8 by 6-inch rectangle, with long side parallel to counter edge.

5 Roll dough away from you into firm cylinder, keeping roll taut by tucking it under itself as you go. Pinch seam closed and place loaf seam side down in prepared pan, pressing dough gently into corners. Cover loosely with greased plastic and let rise until loaf reaches 1 inch above lip of pan and dough springs back minimally when poked gently with your knuckle, 1 to 1½ hours.

6 Adjust oven rack to lower-middle position and heat oven to 350 degrees. Mist loaf with water and bake until deep golden brown and loaf registers 205 to 210 degrees, 35 to 40 minutes, rotating pan halfway through baking. Let loaf cool in pan for 15 minutes. Remove loaf from pan and let cool completely on wire rack, about 3 hours, before serving.

CLASSIC ITALIAN BREAD

makes 1 loaf **food processor size** 11 to 14 cups

why this recipe works You might assume you have to make a trip to a bakery for good Italian bread, but making your own from scratch is surprisingly simple. For a loaf with a crisp crust and a chewy but tender crumb, we started with bread flour. To keep the proofing time short but still get great flavor, we added yeasty tang by using beer as the main liquid. Combining everything in the food processor gave us dough that required only a brief knead by hand. For a nicely browned crust, we baked the loaf on a preheated baking stone. Misting the loaf with water before baking encouraged additional rise and a tender crumb. Use a mild American lager, such as Budweiser; strongly flavored beers will make the bread taste bitter. If you don't have a pizza peel, use an overturned baking sheet covered with a sheet of parchment paper. If you don't have a baking stone, bake the bread on an overturned and preheated rimmed baking sheet. It is important to use chilled beer and ice water in the dough to prevent it from overheating in the food processor.

1 cup mild lager, chilled

6 tablespoons ice water

2 tablespoons extra-virgin olive oil

3 cups (16½ ounces) bread flour

1½ teaspoons instant or rapid-rise yeast

1½ teaspoons salt

1 Whisk beer, water, and oil together in 4-cup liquid measuring cup. Pulse flour, yeast, and salt in food processor until combined, about 5 pulses. With processor running, add beer mixture and process until dough forms rough, elastic ball that begins to clear sides of bowl, 30 seconds to 1 minute.

2 Transfer dough to lightly floured counter. Using your lightly floured hands, knead dough to form smooth, round ball, about 30 seconds. Place dough seam side down in lightly greased large bowl or container, cover tightly with plastic wrap, and let rise until doubled in size, 1 to 1½ hours.

3 Line pizza peel with 16 by 12-inch piece of parchment paper, with long edge of paper perpendicular to handle. Gently press down on dough to deflate any large gas pockets. Turn dough out onto lightly floured counter (side of dough that was against bowl should now be facing up) and press and stretch dough into 10-inch square.

4 Fold top corners of dough diagonally into center of square and press gently to seal. Stretch and fold upper third of dough toward center and press seam gently to seal. Stretch and fold dough in half toward you to form rough loaf and pinch seam closed.

5 Starting at center of dough and working toward ends, gently and evenly roll and stretch dough until it measures 15 inches long by 4 inches wide. Roll loaf seam side down. Gently slide your hands underneath each end of loaf and transfer seam side down to prepared pizza peel.

6 Reshape loaf as needed, tucking edges under to form taut torpedo shape. Cover loosely with greased plastic and let rise until loaf increases in size by about half and dough springs back minimally when poked gently with your knuckle, 30 minutes to 1 hour.

7 One hour before baking, adjust oven rack to lower-middle position, place baking stone on rack, and heat oven to 450 degrees. Using sharp paring knife or single-edge razor blade, make one ½-inch-deep slash with swift, fluid motion lengthwise along top of loaf, starting and stopping about 1½ inches from ends.

8 Mist loaf with water and slide parchment with loaf onto baking stone. Bake until crust is golden brown and loaf registers 205 to 210 degrees, 25 to 30 minutes, rotating loaf halfway through baking. Transfer loaf to wire rack; discard parchment. Let cool completely, about 3 hours, before serving.

RUSTIC WHEAT BERRY BREAD

makes 1 loaf   food processor size 14 cups

why this recipe works We wanted an artisan-style whole-wheat loaf with great flavor and texture. Some artisan bakers go so far as to grind their own flour from whole wheat berries. You might think this sounds a bit unnecessary, and we sure did—until we tried it. Freshly ground wheat berries give bread a robust flavor with superlatively toasty, sweet notes. However, too much whole-wheat flour can also make a bread dense. To solve this problem, we first soaked our wheat berries in water to soften the bran, then ground them to a paste in the food processor. We combined this paste with bread flour and a sponge (a portion of the recipe's flour, yeast, and water that is pre-fermented separate from the rest of the dough), both of which gave the bread better structure. Baking the loaf in the humid environment of a covered Dutch oven helped produce a soft, open crumb and crisp crust. You can find whole wheat berries in the natural or bulk-foods section of the grocery store. If you don't have a baking stone, bake the bread on an overturned and preheated rimmed baking sheet. It is important to use ice water in the dough to prevent it from overheating in the food processor.

soaker

1¼ cups (8 ounces) wheat berries

1 cup water, room temperature

sponge

¾ cup (4⅛ ounces) bread flour

½ cup water, room temperature

¼ teaspoon instant or rapid-rise yeast

dough

¼ cup ice water

1 tablespoon honey

1 cup (5½ ounces) bread flour

2½ teaspoons instant or rapid-rise yeast

1 tablespoon extra-virgin olive oil

1¼ teaspoons salt

1 for the soaker Combine wheat berries and water in bowl, cover tightly with plastic wrap, and let sit at room temperature until grains are fully hydrated and softened, at least 12 hours or up to 24 hours.

2 for the sponge Stir all ingredients together in 4-cup liquid measuring cup with wooden spoon until well combined. Cover tightly with plastic wrap and let sit at room temperature until sponge has risen and begins to collapse, about 6 hours or up to 24 hours.

3 for the dough Process soaked wheat berries and their soaking liquid and ice water in food processor until grains are finely ground and mixture is well combined, about 4 minutes, scraping down sides of bowl as needed. Add sponge and honey and process until just combined, about 10 seconds. Add flour

and yeast and process until dough is just combined and no dry flour remains, about 30 seconds. Let dough rest for 10 minutes.

4 Add oil and salt to dough and process until dough forms rough, elastic ball that begins to clear sides of bowl, 30 seconds to 1 minute. Transfer dough to well-floured counter. Using your well-floured hands, knead dough to form smooth, round ball, about 30 seconds. Place dough seam side down in lightly greased large bowl or container, cover tightly with plastic wrap, and let rise until doubled in size, 1 to 1½ hours.

5 Transfer dough to lightly floured counter (side of dough that was against bowl should now be against counter). Press and stretch dough into 10-inch round, deflating any gas pockets larger than 1 inch. Working around circumference of dough, fold edges toward center until ball forms.

6 Flip dough ball seam side down and, using your cupped hands, drag in small circles on counter until dough feels taut and round and all seams are secured on underside of loaf.

7 Lay 16 by 12-inch sheet of parchment paper on counter and lightly spray with vegetable oil spray. Transfer loaf seam side down to center of prepared parchment. Using parchment as sling, gently lower dough into Dutch oven. Cover tightly with plastic and let rise until loaf increases in size by about half and dough springs back minimally when poked gently with your knuckle, 30 minutes to 1 hour.

8 Adjust oven rack to middle position and heat oven to 450 degrees. Using sharp paring knife or single-edge razor blade, make two 7-inch-long, 1/2-inch-deep slashes with swift, fluid motion on top of loaf to form cross.

9 Cover pot, place in oven, and bake loaf for 30 minutes. Remove lid, reduce oven temperature to 375 degrees, and continue to bake until deep golden brown and loaf registers 205 to 210 degrees, 20 to 25 minutes. Using parchment sling, remove loaf from pot and transfer to wire rack; discard parchment. Let cool completely, about 3 hours, before serving.

THIN-CRUST PIZZA

makes two 13-inch pizzas   **food processor size** 11 to 14 cups

why this recipe works Even the savviest home cooks can struggle to produce the thin, chewy crust of New York–style pizza. We found that the right proportions of high-protein bread flour, water, and yeast produced dough that could be stretched thin but still retained moisture as it baked. We kneaded the wet dough quickly in the food processor, then let it proof in the refrigerator to develop flavor and to keep the air bubbles in the dough tighter so it wouldn't puff up too much in the oven. The processor was also the key to our no-cook pizza sauce and freshly shredded cheese. Placing the baking stone near the top of the oven allowed the top and bottom of the pizza to brown evenly. Many baking stones can crack under the heat of the broiler; be sure to check the manufacturer's website. Our recommended stone, the Old Stone Oven Pizza Baking Stone, can handle the heat of the broiler. You will need a pizza peel for this recipe. It is important to use ice water in the dough to prevent it from overheating in the food processor. Shape the second dough ball while the first pizza bakes, but don't top it until right before you bake it.

dough

3 cups (16½ ounces) bread flour

2 tablespoons sugar

½ teaspoon instant or rapid-rise yeast

1⅓ cups ice water

1 tablespoon vegetable oil

1½ teaspoons salt

sauce and toppings

8 ounces whole-milk mozzarella cheese, chilled

1 (28-ounce) can whole peeled tomatoes, drained with juice reserved

1 tablespoon extra-virgin olive oil

2 garlic cloves, peeled and smashed

1 teaspoon red wine vinegar

1 teaspoon dried oregano

½ teaspoon salt

¼ teaspoon pepper

1 ounce Parmesan cheese, grated fine (½ cup)

1 for the dough Pulse flour, sugar, and yeast in food processor until combined, about 5 pulses. With processor running, add ice water and process until dough is just combined and no dry flour remains, about 10 seconds. Let dough rest for 10 minutes.

2 Add oil and salt to dough and process until dough forms satiny, sticky ball that clears sides of bowl, 30 to 60 seconds. Transfer dough to lightly oiled counter and knead by hand to form smooth, round ball, about 30 seconds. Place dough seam side down in lightly greased large bowl or container, cover tightly with plastic wrap, and refrigerate for at least 24 hours or up to 3 days.

3 for the sauce and toppings Process mozzarella in clean, dry food processor fitted with shredding disk until shredded; set aside. Fit now-empty processor with chopping blade and process tomatoes, oil, garlic, vinegar, oregano, salt, and pepper until smooth, about 30 seconds. Transfer mixture to 2-cup liquid measuring cup and add reserved tomato juice until sauce measures 2 cups. Reserve 1 cup sauce; set aside remaining sauce for another use.

4 Press down on dough to deflate. Transfer dough to clean counter, divide in half, and cover loosely with greased plastic. Pat 1 piece of dough (keep remaining piece covered) into 4-inch round. Working around circumference of dough, fold edges toward center until ball forms.

5 Flip ball seam side down and, using your cupped hands, drag in small circles on counter until dough feels taut and round and all seams are secured on underside. (If dough sticks to your hands, lightly dust top of dough with flour.)

Repeat with remaining piece of dough. Space dough balls 3 inches apart, cover loosely with greased plastic, and let rest for 1 hour.

6 Meanwhile, adjust oven rack 4 inches from broiler element, set baking stone on rack, and heat oven to 500 degrees for 1 hour, then heat broiler for 10 minutes. Coat 1 dough ball generously with flour and place on well-floured counter. Using your fingertips, gently flatten into 8-inch round, leaving 1 inch of outer edge slightly thicker than center. Using your hands, gently stretch dough into 12-inch round, working along edge and giving disk quarter-turns.

7 Transfer dough to well-floured pizza peel and stretch into 13-inch round. Using back of spoon or ladle, spread ½ cup tomato sauce in even layer over surface of dough, leaving ¼-inch border around edge. Sprinkle ¼ cup Parmesan evenly over sauce, followed by 1 cup mozzarella.

8 Slide pizza carefully onto baking stone and return oven to 500 degrees. Bake until crust is well browned and cheese is bubbly and partially browned, 8 to 10 minutes, rotating pizza halfway through baking. Transfer pizza to wire rack and let cool for 5 minutes before slicing and serving. Heat broiler for 10 minutes. Repeat with remaining dough, sauce, and toppings, returning oven to 500 degrees when pizza is placed on stone.

SPINACH-RICOTTA CALZONES

serves 4   food processor size 11 to 14 cups

why this recipe works Pizzerias often serve up giant, unappealing calzones with wet fillings and bready crusts. In our experience, the only calzone worth eating is one made at home. To develop our version, we took serious advantage of our food processor, which was able to perfectly chop and mix the filling and create springy pizza dough in a snap. However, regular pizza dough just didn't cut it; it made bloated, misshapen calzones with unacceptable air bubbles. After reducing the amount of water in the mixture, we got what we were after: dough that was easy to shape around the filling and that baked up chewy and crisp. For our flavorful filling, we used a base of spinach and creamy ricotta to which we added an egg yolk to thicken the mixture, a bit of oil for richness, and two more cheeses: easy-melting mozzarella and nutty-tasting Parmesan. We spread the filling onto the bottom halves of the two rolled-out dough rounds and then brushed an egg wash on the edges before folding the top halves over and sealing the dough so it would stay closed as the calzones baked. Cutting vents in the tops allowed excess moisture in the filling to escape during baking so the crust didn't become soggy. After the calzones baked for just 15 minutes, we let them cool briefly on a wire rack to keep the bottoms crisp. It is important to use ice water in the dough to prevent it from overheating in the food processor. Serve the calzones with your favorite marinara sauce.

dough

2 cups (11 ounces) plus 2 tablespoons bread flour

1⅛ teaspoons instant or rapid-rise yeast

¾ teaspoon salt

1 tablespoon extra-virgin olive oil

¾ cup ice water

filling

10 ounces frozen chopped spinach, thawed and squeezed dry

4 ounces mozzarella cheese, cut into ½-inch pieces (1 cup)

8 ounces (1 cup) whole-milk ricotta cheese

1 ounce Parmesan cheese, grated (½ cup)

1 tablespoon extra-virgin olive oil

1 large egg yolk

2 garlic cloves, peeled and smashed

1 tablespoon fresh oregano leaves

¼ teaspoon salt

⅛ teaspoon red pepper flakes

1 large egg, lightly beaten with 1 tablespoon water and pinch salt

1 for the dough Pulse flour, yeast, and salt in food processor until combined, about 5 pulses. With processor running, add oil, then ice water, and process until rough, elastic ball that begins to clear sides of bowl forms, 30 to 40 seconds. Let dough rest for 2 minutes, then process for 30 seconds longer.

2 Transfer dough to lightly floured counter and using your lightly floured hands, knead to form smooth, round ball, about 30 seconds. Place dough seam side down in lightly greased large bowl or container, cover tightly with plastic wrap, and let rise until doubled in size, 1½ to 2 hours. (Unrisen dough can be refrigerated for up to 16 hours; let sit at room temperature for 30 minutes before shaping in step 4.)

3 for the filling Adjust oven rack to lower-middle position and heat oven to 500 degrees. Cut two 9-inch square pieces of parchment paper. Process spinach, mozzarella, ricotta, Parmesan, oil, egg yolk, garlic, oregano, salt, and pepper flakes in clean, dry processor until combined, about 8 pulses.

4 Press down on dough to deflate. Transfer dough to lightly floured counter, divide in half, and cover loosely with greased plastic. Press and roll 1 piece of dough (keep remaining piece covered) into 9-inch round of even thickness. Transfer to parchment square and reshape as needed. Repeat with remaining piece of dough.

5 Spread half of spinach filling evenly over half of each dough round, leaving 1-inch border at edge. Brush edges with egg mixture. Fold other half of dough over filling, leaving ½-inch border of bottom half uncovered.

6 Press edges of dough together, pressing out any air pockets in calzones. Starting at 1 end of calzone, place your index finger diagonally across edge, pull bottom layer of dough over tip of your finger, and press to seal.

7 Using sharp knife or single-edge razor blade, cut 5 steam vents, about 1½ inches long, in tops of calzones. Brush tops with remaining egg mixture. Transfer calzones (still on parchment) to rimmed baking sheet, trimming parchment as needed to fit. Bake until golden brown, about 15 minutes, rotating sheet halfway through baking. Transfer calzones to wire rack and discard parchment. Let cool for 10 minutes before serving.

MONKEY BREAD

makes 1 loaf   **food processor size** 14 cups

why this recipe works Monkey bread is a knotty-looking loaf made from rich balls of dough coated with cinnamon, sugar, and melted butter and baked in a Bundt pan. It's traditionally served warm so that the sticky baked pieces can be pulled apart. We wanted a fast recipe that didn't compromise on the delicious flavor and sticky, sweet appeal of this treat. To help make this recipe more approachable, we mixed and kneaded the dough in the food processor, which combined the dry and wet ingredients into a springy dough in about a minute. To expedite the rising and proofing process, we used a generous amount of instant yeast and added sugar to the dough, which jumpstarted the yeast. Butter and milk helped keep the dough tender and flavorful. Before assembling the bread, we rolled the balls of dough in melted butter and sugar to give them a thick, caramel-like coating. White sugar was good, but light brown sugar, with its molasses notes, made the coating even better. A generous amount of cinnamon added warm character. Once the bread had cooled slightly, we finished by drizzling a simple confectioners' sugar glaze over the top. It is important to use chilled milk and ice water in the dough to prevent it from overheating in the food processor.

dough

1 cup whole milk, chilled

⅓ cup ice water

3¼ cups (16¼ ounces) all-purpose flour

¼ cup (1¾ ounces) granulated sugar

2¼ teaspoons instant or rapid-rise yeast

2 teaspoons salt

2 tablespoons unsalted butter, melted

brown sugar coating

1 cup packed (7 ounces) light brown sugar

2 teaspoons ground cinnamon

8 tablespoons unsalted butter, melted and cooled

glaze

1 cup (4 ounces) confectioners' sugar

2 tablespoons whole milk

1 for the dough Whisk milk and ice water together in 4-cup liquid measuring cup. Pulse flour, sugar, yeast, and salt in food processor until combined, about 5 pulses. With processor running, add milk mixture, then melted butter, and process until dough forms rough, sticky ball, about 30 seconds.

2 Using rubber spatula, transfer dough to lightly floured counter. Using your lightly floured hands, knead dough to form smooth, round ball, about 30 seconds. Place dough seam side down in lightly greased large bowl or container, cover tightly with plastic wrap, and let rise until doubled in size,

1½ to 2 hours. (Unrisen dough can be refrigerated for up to 16 hours; let sit at room temperature for 1 hour before shaping in step 4.)

3 for the brown sugar coating Thoroughly grease 12-cup nonstick Bundt pan. Combine sugar and cinnamon in medium bowl. Place melted butter in second bowl.

4 Transfer dough to lightly floured counter and press into rough 8-inch square. Using pizza cutter or chef's knife, cut dough into 8 even strips. Cut each strip into 8 pieces (64 pieces total). Cover loosely with greased plastic.

5 Working with a few pieces of dough at a time (keep remaining pieces covered), place on clean counter and, using your cupped hand, drag in small circles until dough feels taut and round. Dip balls in melted butter, then roll in sugar mixture to coat. Place balls in prepared pan, staggering seams where dough balls meet as you build layers.

6 Cover pan tightly with plastic and let rise until dough balls reach 1 to 2 inches below lip of pan, 1½ to 2 hours.

7 Adjust oven rack to middle position and heat oven to 350 degrees. Bake bread until top is deep golden brown and caramel begins to bubble around edges, 30 to 35 minutes. Let bread cool in pan for 5 minutes, then invert onto serving platter and let cool for 10 minutes.

8 for the glaze Meanwhile, whisk sugar and milk together in bowl until smooth. Drizzle glaze over bread, letting it run down sides. Serve warm.

YEASTED DOUGHNUTS

makes 16 doughnuts and doughnut holes   **food processor size** 11 to 14 cups

why this recipe works We set out to develop a recipe for yeasted doughnuts that we could make fresh at home without any need for a commercial deep-fat fryer. Yeasted doughnuts are simply enriched bread dough that's rolled, cut into circles, and fried. What we wanted was a lightly sweetened doughnut that was tender on the inside and lightly crisp on the outside. All-purpose flour in the dough yielded a light, fluffy interior. The dough came together quickly in the food processor and chilled milk (instead of the usual room-temperature milk used in other baking recipes) helped keep the butter from getting too soft during mixing. Because we wanted the flavor of the doughnuts to complement a variety of additional glazes and coatings, we didn't make the dough too sweet. Less sugar also made the doughnuts less likely to brown too quickly in the hot oil and end up burnt. We also kept the amount of butter in check to avoid overly rich, greasy doughnuts. If you don't have a doughnut cutter, you can use a biscuit cutter (about 2½ inches) for the doughnuts, and a smaller one (about 1¼ inches) for the holes. Use a Dutch oven that holds 6 quarts or more for this recipe. It is important to use chilled milk in the dough to prevent it from overheating in the food processor. The doughnuts are best eaten the day they are made.

⅔ cup whole milk, chilled

2 large eggs

3 cups (15 ounces) all-purpose flour

6 tablespoons (2⅔ ounces) sugar, plus 1 cup for rolling

2¼ teaspoons instant or rapid-rise yeast

½ teaspoon salt

6 tablespoons unsalted butter, cut into 6 pieces and softened

2 quarts vegetable oil

1 Whisk milk and eggs together in 4-cup liquid measuring cup until combined. Pulse flour, 6 tablespoons sugar, yeast, and salt in food processor until combined, about 5 pulses. With processor running, add milk mixture, then butter, and process until dough forms rough, sticky ball, about 30 seconds.

2 Using rubber spatula, transfer dough to lightly floured counter. Using your lightly floured hands, knead dough to form smooth, round ball, about 30 seconds. Place dough seam side down in lightly greased large bowl or container, cover tightly with plastic wrap, and let rise until nearly doubled in size, 2 to 2½ hours. (Unrisen dough can be refrigerated for up to 16 hours; let sit at room temperature for 1 hour before rolling in step 4.)

3 Set wire rack in rimmed baking sheet. Line second sheet with parchment paper and dust lightly with flour. Press down on dough to deflate, then transfer to lightly floured counter.

4 Press and roll dough into 12-inch round, about ½ inch thick. Cut dough using 2½- or 3-inch doughnut cutter, gathering scraps and rerolling them as needed. Place doughnut rings and holes on floured sheet, cover loosely with greased plastic, and let rise until puffy, 30 to 45 minutes.

5 Add oil to large Dutch oven until it measures about 1½ inches deep and heat over medium-high heat to 375 degrees. Working in batches of 4 dough holes and 4 dough rings at a time, fry until golden brown, about 30 seconds per side for holes and 45 to 60 seconds per side for doughnuts. Using wire skimmer or slotted spoon, transfer doughnuts and doughnut holes to prepared wire rack.

6 Spread remaining 1 cup sugar in shallow dish. Let doughnuts and doughnut holes cool for 10 minutes, then roll in sugar to coat. Serve warm or at room temperature.

YEASTED CINNAMON-SUGAR DOUGHNUTS

Combine 1 tablespoon ground cinnamon with the sugar before rolling doughnuts and doughnut holes in step 6.

YEASTED VANILLA-GLAZED DOUGHNUTS

Omit 1 cup sugar for rolling. While doughnuts are cooling, whisk together ½ cup half-and-half, 3 cups confectioners' sugar, sifted, and 1 teaspoon vanilla extract in medium bowl until combined. When doughnuts have cooled, dip 1 side of each doughnut into glaze, let excess drip off, and transfer to wire rack. Let glaze set, about 15 minutes, before serving.

YEASTED CHOCOLATE-GLAZED DOUGHNUTS

Omit 1 cup sugar for rolling. While doughnuts are cooling, place 4 ounces finely chopped semisweet or bittersweet chocolate in small bowl. Add ½ cup hot half-and-half and whisk together to melt chocolate. Add 2 cups confectioners' sugar, sifted, and whisk until no lumps remain. When doughnuts have cooled, dip 1 side of each doughnut into glaze, let excess drip off, and transfer to wire rack. Let glaze set, about 15 minutes, before serving.

HOMEMADE FRESH PASTA WITH TOMATO-BROWN BUTTER SAUCE

serves 4 to 6   food processor size 11 to 14 cups

why this recipe works Dried pasta is convenient, but it can't compare to the texture and chew of fresh pasta. We wanted a foolproof recipe for homemade fresh pasta that didn't require any special equipment, but rolling out traditional pasta dough by hand is no easy task. To make a more pliable dough, we added extra fat to the traditional flour-egg pasta dough, in the form of olive oil, plus even more fat and protein from 6 extra egg yolks. Resting the dough after mixing it in the food processor made it even more malleable. A simple rolling and cutting technique gave us perfect fresh pasta. We also used the food processor to make a simple tomato sauce. If using a high-protein all-purpose flour like King Arthur brand, increase the number of egg yolks to 7. The longer the dough rests in step 2, the easier it will be to roll out. When rolling out the dough, avoid adding too much extra flour, which may result in excessive snapback. This pasta can also be served with our Classic Pesto (page 24), Mushroom Bolognese (page 77), or 3 cups of your favorite homemade sauce.

pasta
2 cups (10 ounces) all-purpose flour

2 large eggs plus 6 large yolks

2 tablespoons olive oil

1 tablespoon salt

sauce
1 (28-ounce) can whole peeled tomatoes

4 tablespoons unsalted butter, cut into 4 pieces

2 garlic cloves, minced

½ teaspoon sugar

Salt and pepper

2 teaspoons sherry vinegar

3 tablespoons chopped fresh basil

Grated Parmesan cheese

1 for the pasta Process flour, eggs and yolks, and oil in food processor until mixture forms cohesive dough that feels soft and is barely tacky to touch, about 45 seconds. (If dough sticks to fingers, add up to ¼ cup flour, 1 tablespoon at a time, until barely tacky. If dough doesn't become cohesive, add up to 1 tablespoon water, 1 teaspoon at a time, until it just comes together; process 30 seconds longer.)

2 Turn dough ball onto dry surface and knead until smooth, 1 to 2 minutes. Shape dough into 6-inch-long cylinder. Wrap with plastic wrap and set aside at room temperature to rest for at least 1 hour or up to 4 hours.

3 Cut cylinder crosswise into 6 equal pieces. Working with 1 piece of dough at a time (rewrap remaining dough), dust both sides with flour, place cut side down on clean work surface, and press into 3-inch square. Using heavy rolling pin, roll into 6-inch square. Dust both sides of dough lightly with flour. Starting at center of square, roll dough away from you in 1 motion. Return rolling pin to center of dough and roll toward you in 1 motion. Repeat steps of rolling until dough sticks to counter and measures roughly 12 inches long. Lightly dust both sides of dough with flour and continue rolling dough until it measures roughly 20 inches long and 6 inches wide, frequently lifting dough to release it from counter. (You should be able to easily see outline of your fingers through dough.) If dough firmly sticks to counter and wrinkles when rolled out, dust dough lightly with flour.

4 Transfer pasta sheet to kitchen towel and let stand, uncovered, until firm around edges, about 15 minutes; meanwhile, roll out remaining dough. Starting with 1 short end, gently fold pasta sheet at 2-inch intervals until sheet has been folded into flat, rectangular roll. With sharp chef's knife,

slice crosswise into ³⁄₁₆-inch-thick noodles. Use fingers to unfurl pasta and transfer to baking sheet. Repeat folding and cutting remaining sheets of dough. Set pasta aside while making sauce; pasta should be cooked within 1 hour of cutting. (Pasta can be frozen on baking sheet until firm, then transferred to zipper-lock bag and stored for up to 2 weeks; cook pasta straight from freezer as directed in step 6.)

5 for the sauce Process tomatoes and their juice in clean, dry processor until smooth, about 30 seconds. Melt 3 tablespoons butter in 12-inch skillet over medium-high heat, swirling occasionally, until butter is dark brown and releases nutty aroma, about 1½ minutes. Stir in garlic and cook for

10 seconds. Stir in tomatoes, sugar, and ½ teaspoon salt, and simmer until sauce is slightly reduced, about 8 minutes. Off heat, whisk in remaining 1 tablespoon butter and vinegar. Season with salt and pepper to taste; cover to keep warm.

6 Bring 4 quarts water to boil in large Dutch oven. Add 1 tablespoon salt and pasta and cook until tender but still al dente, about 3 minutes. Reserve ½ cup cooking water, then drain pasta and transfer to skillet with sauce. Add ¼ cup reserved cooking water to pasta and cook over medium heat, tossing constantly, until hot and well coated with sauce. Adjust consistency with remaining reserved cooking water as needed. Off heat, stir in basil and season with salt and pepper to taste. Serve with Parmesan.

EMBRACE ALMOST-NO-BOWL BAKING

When you eliminate the hand stirring and piles of dirty dishes, baked goods of all kinds become more appealing everyday projects. The food processor famously tackles pie crust in minutes, but we were surprised at how well it did with cookies and brownies, and even breakfast breads and a frosted layer cake. Avoiding overmixing proved less of a hurdle than we anticipated with a little tinkering. A great bonus was the ease with which we could prepare and incorporate mix-ins like shredded cheese, sliced fruit, grated vegetables, and chopped nuts, all featured here. Mixing up the flavors of a basic recipe takes hardly any extra effort when you're baking with your food processor.

FOOD PROCESSOR FINDINGS

Here are a few tricks we've discovered for making baking simpler with your food processor:

1 The key to adapting many baking recipes for the food processor is to reconsider the order in which ingredients are added. Because the processor makes mixing so quick, ingredients that need time to start working, like leaveners, should be added earlier than usual. Conversely, flour should be added toward the end of mixing to avoid overdeveloping the gluten, which can lead to tough baked goods.

2 Shredding and slicing fruits and vegetables in the food processor are a cinch, but these ingredients contain a lot of water, so we often drain them for recipes like our Zucchini Bread (page 131), or precook them as for our Classic Apple Pie (page 144).

3 The food processor is an ideal tool for cutting fat into flour to make tender, flaky pie and tart doughs, and because the processor works so quickly, the fat doesn't have time to get soft or melt.

4 When you chop or grind nuts in the food processor, the heat from the grinding process helps release the nuts' volatile oils for more fragrant, flavorful results.

FLOUR + BUTTER + PROCESSOR = BAKED GOOD PERFECTION

Butter is integral to great biscuits and pie crusts because when it's heated, the water in it turns to steam, which lifts the dough and creates a flaky texture. But for this to work, the butter must be evenly dispersed in layers throughout the dough. This way, when the butter melts, the steam separates the dough into superthin layers. The butter also has to melt in the oven, not during mixing. To help with this, we like to use chilled butter in our doughs, but to make it even more foolproof, we turn to the food processor. Because the processor can cut butter into flour more quickly than other methods, there's less chance of the butter getting overly softened or even melting during mixing, and it gets worked in more evenly than it would if this step was done by hand.

**oversoftened butter
(flat and dense)**

**just-right butter
(perfect flaky layers)**

LIGHT AND FLUFFY BUTTERMILK BISCUITS

makes 12 biscuits **food processor size** 7 to 14 cups

why this recipe works Although biscuits may seem like one of the simplest baked goods you can make, there are plenty of ways they can go wrong. Bad biscuits can be greasy, tough, and pretty much inedible. To ensure that ours were light and fluffy as well as tender and flavorful, we began by chilling a combination of butter and shortening. Chilling the fats ensured that they melted in the oven, not during mixing, thus creating the pockets of steam required for flaky results. Using the food processor to quickly cut the fat into the dry ingredients also helped keep the butter and shortening from getting too soft. We then stirred in the buttermilk by hand to ensure that the ingredients were uniformly combined without overmixing the dough, which can lead to toughness. The dough required only a tiny bit of hand kneading to develop the gluten essential for fluffy biscuits. After rolling and stamping the dough, we placed the biscuits upside down on the baking sheet; with the flat underside on top, the biscuits rose tall and even. A hot oven jump-started the rising process, and we then turned the heat down to finish baking without burning the biscuits. For a variation that mixed things up, we combined the subtle nuttiness of Parmesan and the mellow spice of black pepper to create a pleasingly sophisticated flavor profile.

3 cups (15 ounces) all-purpose flour

1 tablespoon sugar

1 tablespoon baking powder

½ teaspoon baking soda

1 teaspoon salt

8 tablespoons unsalted butter, cut into ½-inch pieces and chilled

4 tablespoons vegetable shortening, cut into ½-inch pieces and chilled

1¼ cups buttermilk

1 Adjust oven rack to middle position and heat oven to 450 degrees. Line rimmed baking sheet with parchment paper. Pulse flour, sugar, baking powder, baking soda, and salt in food processor until combined, about 5 pulses. Sprinkle chilled butter and shortening over top and pulse until mixture resembles coarse meal, about 15 pulses.

2 Transfer flour mixture to large bowl and stir in buttermilk until just incorporated; do not overmix. Turn dough out onto lightly floured counter and knead briefly, 8 to 10 times, to form smooth, cohesive ball.

3 Roll dough into 9-inch circle, about ¾ inch thick. Cut biscuits into rounds using 2½-inch biscuit cutter, dipping cutter in flour as needed. Gather dough scraps together, pat gently into ¾-inch-thick circle, and cut out additional rounds. Place biscuits upside down on prepared sheet. (Raw biscuits can be refrigerated for up to 1 day; bake as directed.)

4 Bake until biscuits begin to rise, about 5 minutes. Rotate sheet, reduce oven temperature to 400 degrees, and continue to bake until golden brown, 10 to 12 minutes. Transfer biscuits to wire rack, let cool for 5 minutes, and serve.

BUTTERMILK BISCUITS WITH PARMESAN AND BLACK PEPPER
Add ¾ cup grated Parmesan cheese and 1 teaspoon coarsely ground black pepper to processor with flour.

QUICK CHEESE BREAD

makes 1 loaf **food processor size** 7 to 14 cups

why this recipe works Sometimes you want a crusty, savory loaf of bread without all the work of rising and kneading that goes into a yeasted dough. This is where quick breads come in. Cheese bread is one of our favorite simple batter breads, and using the food processor makes it even easier. Our version gets its flavor from a combination of Parmesan and cheddar cheeses and its rise from a generous amount of baking powder instead of yeast. We started by using the food processor to shred Parmesan, which went on the bottom of the pan and the top of the loaf to create a crisp, savory crust. Then we simply combined the wet ingredients (including sour cream for flavor and moisture and melted butter for richness) and the dry ingredients in the processor. We added the flour last to avoid overworking the gluten in the dough. Big chunks of cheddar cheese pulsed into the mixture ensured pockets of rich, salty flavor throughout the loaf. You can substitute a mild Asiago, crumbled into ¼- to ½-inch pieces, for the cheddar. (Aged Asiago that is as firm as Parmesan is too sharp and piquant.) The test kitchen's preferred loaf pan measures 8½ by 4½ inches; if you use a 9 by 5-inch loaf pan, start checking for doneness 5 minutes earlier than advised in the recipe. If, when testing the bread for doneness, the skewer comes out with what looks like uncooked batter clinging to it, try again in a different but still central spot. (A skewer hitting a pocket of cheese may give a false indication.) The texture of this bread improves as it cools, so resist the urge to slice the loaf when it's still warm.

3 ounces Parmesan cheese	1 tablespoon baking powder	4 ounces extra-sharp cheddar cheese, cut into ½-inch pieces (1 cup)
1 cup whole milk	1 teaspoon salt	
½ cup sour cream	⅛ teaspoon pepper	
1 large egg	⅛ teaspoon cayenne pepper	
3 tablespoons unsalted butter, melted	2½ cups (12½ ounces) all-purpose flour	

1 Adjust oven rack to middle position and heat oven to 350 degrees. Using food processor fitted with shredding disk, process Parmesan until shredded (you should have about 1 cup). Grease 8½ by 4½-inch loaf pan, then sprinkle ½ cup Parmesan evenly in bottom of pan; set aside remaining Parmesan.

2 Fit now-empty processor with chopping blade and process milk, sour cream, egg, melted butter, baking powder, salt, pepper, and cayenne until combined, about 10 seconds, scraping down sides of bowl as needed. Add flour and cheddar and pulse until just incorporated, about 5 pulses. (Batter will be heavy and thick; do not overmix).

3 Transfer batter to prepared pan, smooth top, and sprinkle with remaining ½ cup Parmesan. Bake loaf until golden brown and skewer inserted in center comes out clean, 45 to 50 minutes, rotating pan halfway through baking.

4 Let loaf cool in pan on wire rack for 15 minutes. Remove loaf from pan and let cool completely on rack, about 2 hours. Serve.

ZUCCHINI BREAD

makes 1 loaf **food processor size** 7 to 14 cups

why this recipe works Zucchini bread is a classic way to use up extra summer produce, but most recipes call for only a minimal amount of zucchini and result in a loaf with a dense, under-baked texture. Seeking to pack in double the amount of zucchini typically used, we developed a zucchini bread with rich flavor and a moist—not soggy—texture that we couldn't wait to eat. The key proved to be removing as much moisture as possible from the zucchini, which enabled us to use a full 1½ pounds of it without compromising the texture of the bread. Our food processor method really streamlined the process: it shredded the zucchini, chopped the nuts, and then mixed the batter. To banish the gumminess sometimes associated with zucchini bread, we added a little whole-wheat flour, which is more absorbent than white flour. It easily soaked up any remaining liquid, giving the bread a much better structure. As a bonus, the wheat flour contributed a great hearty flavor that perfectly complemented the rustic loaf. The addition of warm spices elevated the bread, and a little vanilla extract helped to round out the flavor profile. Toasted walnuts added along with the shredded zucchini provided a pleasant contrast in texture. For a finishing touch, we sprinkled a generous amount of sugar on top of the batter in the pan, which then baked into a sweet, crisp crust. The test kitchen's preferred loaf pan measures 8½ by 4½ inches; if you use a 9 by 5-inch loaf pan, start checking for doneness 5 minutes earlier than advised in the recipe.

1½ pounds zucchini, trimmed

1¼ cups packed (8¾ ounces) brown sugar

2 large eggs

¼ cup vegetable oil

1 tablespoon ground cinnamon

1½ teaspoons salt

1 teaspoon vanilla extract

1 teaspoon baking powder

1 teaspoon baking soda

½ teaspoon ground nutmeg

¾ cup walnuts, toasted

1½ cups (7½ ounces) all-purpose flour

½ cup (2¾ ounces) whole-wheat flour

1 tablespoon granulated sugar

1 Adjust oven rack to middle position and heat oven to 325 degrees. Grease 8½ by 4½-inch loaf pan. Working in batches, use food processor fitted with shredding disk to process zucchini until shredded. Place half of shredded zucchini in center of dish towel. Gather ends together and twist tightly to drain as much liquid as possible, discarding liquid. Repeat with remaining zucchini. (You should have ½ to ⅔ cup liquid total.)

2 Fit now-empty processor with chopping blade and process brown sugar, eggs, oil, cinnamon, salt, vanilla, baking powder, baking soda, and nutmeg until combined, about 10 seconds, scraping down sides of bowl as needed. Add zucchini and walnuts and pulse until combined, about 5 pulses. Add allpurpose flour and whole-wheat flour and pulse until just incorporated, about 5 pulses; do not overmix.

3 Transfer batter to prepared pan, smooth top, and sprinkle with granulated sugar. Bake loaf until top bounces back when gently pressed and skewer inserted in center comes out with few moist crumbs attached, 65 to 75 minutes, rotating pan halfway through baking.

4 Let loaf cool in pan on wire rack for 15 minutes. Remove loaf from pan and let cool completely on rack, about 2 hours. Serve.

APPLE-CINNAMON MUFFINS

makes 12 muffins   **food processor size** 7 to 14 cups

why this recipe works The key to building big apple flavor in a tender muffin lies in the technique. We started by shredding tart Granny Smith apples in the food processor and then wringing them out to remove as much excess liquid as possible. We reserved that juice (and all its fresh apple flavor) to add back to the batter in a measured amount later, which gave us control over the moisture in the muffins. Using shredded fruit ensured that there was plenty of apple in each and every bite. Yogurt added a nice tang without contributing too much extra moisture, which could lead to soggy muffins, plus cinnamon for a pleasant spice note. We used the food processor to both shred the apples and mix the batter, making sure to add the apples and flour last to avoid overprocessing. For a finishing touch we sprinkled the muffins with a cinnamon-sugar mixture, which made for a sweet, crackly top and reinforced the warm spice flavors. Make sure to spray the muffin tin thoroughly, inside the cups and on top.

topping

2 tablespoons granulated sugar

2 tablespoons packed brown sugar

¼ teaspoon ground cinnamon

muffins

2 Granny Smith apples, peeled, cored, and halved

1 cup (7 ounces) granulated sugar

½ cup plain whole-milk yogurt

2 large eggs

4 tablespoons unsalted butter, melted

¼ cup vegetable oil

2 tablespoons packed brown sugar

2½ teaspoons baking powder

¼ teaspoon baking soda

1¼ teaspoons salt

1 teaspoon vanilla extract

¾ teaspoon ground cinnamon

2½ cups (12½ ounces) all-purpose flour

1 for the topping Using your fingers, combine granulated sugar, brown sugar, and cinnamon in bowl; cover and set aside.

2 for the muffins Adjust oven rack to middle position and heat oven to 400 degrees. Thoroughly grease 12-cup muffin tin. Using food processor fitted with shredding disk, process apples until shredded. Place shredded apples in center of dish towel. Gather ends together and twist tightly to drain as much juice as possible, reserving juice. You should have about ½ cup juice; add water, if needed, to make ½ cup.

3 Fit now-empty processor with chopping blade and process reserved juice, granulated sugar, yogurt, eggs, melted butter, oil, brown sugar, baking powder, baking soda, salt, vanilla, and cinnamon until combined, about 10 seconds, scraping down sides of bowl as needed. Add apples and pulse until combined, about 2 pulses. Add flour and pulse until just incorporated, about 5 pulses; do not overmix.

4 Divide batter evenly among prepared muffin cups (cups will be filled to rim) and sprinkle with topping. Bake muffins until golden brown and toothpick inserted in center comes out with few crumbs attached, 18 to 22 minutes, rotating muffin tin halfway through baking.

5 Let muffins cool in muffin tin on wire rack for 10 minutes. Remove muffins from muffin tin and let cool on rack for 5 minutes longer. Serve warm or at room temperature.

COFFEE CAKE WITH PECAN-CINNAMON STREUSEL

serves 8 to 10   food processor size 7 to 14 cups

why this recipe works The major appeal of coffee cake comes from the nutty crunch of the topping in contrast with the moist cake. The trouble is, many recipes for this simple baked good are relatively complicated, requiring multiple bowls and appliances. We wanted a simpler method that still produced the same tender cake and crunchy, flavorful topping. Of course, the food processor was the natural solution. It was the perfect tool both for prepping ingredients like the chopped nuts and for creating the cake. For the cake, we used a reverse creaming method: First, we worked the butter into the dry ingredients, then we mixed in the wet ingredients. Combining the flour and butter first helped limit the amount of gluten that could be formed, so the cake stayed soft and tender. The processor also made the streusel topping in just seconds for a one-tool take on classic coffee cake that offered an appealing combination of crunchy cinnamon-pecan streusel and moist, rich cake in every bite. Avoid testing this cake for doneness with a skewer until the center appears firm when the pan is shaken as this can cause the center of the cake to sink.

streusel

1 cup pecans, toasted

⅓ cup packed (2⅓ ounces) brown sugar

½ cup (2½ ounces) all-purpose flour

¾ teaspoon ground cinnamon

¼ teaspoon salt

4 tablespoons unsalted butter, melted and cooled

1 teaspoon water

cake

1⅔ cups (8⅓ ounces) all-purpose flour

1 cup (7 ounces) granulated sugar

1 teaspoon ground cinnamon

1 teaspoon baking powder

½ teaspoon baking soda

¾ teaspoon salt

7 tablespoons unsalted butter, cut into 7 pieces and softened

¾ cup whole milk

1 large egg plus 1 large yolk

1 teaspoon vanilla extract

1 for the streusel Process pecans and sugar in food processor until finely ground, about 10 seconds. Add flour, cinnamon, and salt and pulse until combined, about 5 pulses. Add butter and water and pulse until butter is fully incorporated and mixture begins to form clumps, 8 to 10 pulses; set aside.

2 for the cake Adjust oven rack to lower-middle position and heat oven to 350 degrees. Grease and flour 9-inch springform pan. Place pan in rimmed baking sheet. Pulse flour, sugar, cinnamon, baking powder, baking soda, and salt in now-empty processor until combined, about 5 pulses. Add butter and pulse until very small but visible pieces of butter remain, about 20 pulses. Add milk, egg and yolk, and vanilla and pulse until dry ingredients are moistened, about

5 pulses, scraping down sides of bowl as needed. Continue to pulse until mixture is well combined, about 5 pulses (some small pieces of butter will remain).

3 Transfer batter to prepared pan and smooth top. Starting at edges of pan, sprinkle streusel in even layer over batter. Bake cake in sheet until center is firm and skewer inserted in center comes out clean, 45 to 55 minutes.

4 Transfer cake from sheet to wire rack and let cool in pan for 15 minutes. Remove sides of pan and let cake cool completely on rack, about 2 hours. Use offset spatula to transfer cake to serving platter. Serve.

EASY POUND CAKE

serves 8   **food processor size** 7 to 14 cups

why this recipe works Pound cake should be the ultimate easy cake—after all, it calls for just a handful of ingredients. The problem is that most recipes use a finicky mixing method in which all the ingredients need to be the same temperature; otherwise the batter turns into a curdled mess—and there's no way to save it. Looking for an easier way, we found the answers to our fussy batter problems: hot melted (rather than softened) butter and the food processor. The fast-moving blade of the processor, in conjunction with the hot butter, emulsified the liquid ingredients quickly before they had a chance to curdle. Plus, it sped up the process so the cake could be in the oven (and on a plate) that much sooner. It also made it super simple to add fresh lemon flavor for an easy variation. The test kitchen's preferred loaf pan measures 8½ by 4½ inches; if you use a 9 by 5-inch loaf pan, start checking for doneness 5 minutes earlier than advised in the recipe.

1¼ cups (8¾ ounces) sugar

4 large eggs, room temperature

1½ teaspoons vanilla extract

1 teaspoon baking powder

½ teaspoon salt

16 tablespoons unsalted butter, melted and hot

1½ cups (6 ounces) cake flour

1 Adjust oven rack to middle position and heat oven to 350 degrees. Grease and flour 8½ by 4½-inch loaf pan. Process sugar, eggs, vanilla, baking powder, and salt in food processor until combined, about 10 seconds, scraping down sides of bowl as needed. With processor running, slowly add hot melted butter until incorporated, about 10 seconds. Add flour and pulse until just incorporated, about 5 pulses; do not overmix.

2 Transfer batter to prepared pan and smooth top. Gently tap pan on counter to release air bubbles. Bake cake until skewer inserted in center comes out with few moist crumbs attached, 50 to 60 minutes, rotating pan halfway through baking.

3 Let cake cool in pan on wire rack for 15 minutes. Remove cake from pan and let cool completely on rack, about 2 hours. Serve.

EASY LEMON POUND CAKE

Add 2 tablespoons grated lemon zest (2 lemons) and 2 teaspoons juice to processor with sugar.

CARROT LAYER CAKE

serves 10 to 12   **food processor size** 9 to 14 cups

why this recipe works When done right, carrot cake can be a rich, delicious treat: a perfect combination of sweet carrots, spiced cake, and tangy cream cheese frosting. However, turning this classic into a showstopping layer cake comes with some challenges. First, there's the mere task of grating all the carrots required for a really distinctive carrot cake. Then there's the issue of successfully stacking layers of heavy, moist cake and fluffy frosting; and of course all these separate steps usually create a giant mess of dirty bowls, spoons, and other tools. The food processor helped us make light work of the whole process. We started with the carrots. We wanted a cake loaded with sweet carrot flavor, so we shredded a full pound of carrots using the shredding disk of the processor. We then mixed up a basic cake batter right in the processor bowl, amping up the flavor with healthy doses of cinnamon, nutmeg, and cloves. We pulsed the carrots back in just before adding the flour, which guaranteed that they would be evenly dispersed and the batter would not get overworked. While the layers baked, we whipped up a simple cream cheese frosting in the processor with vanilla and plenty of confectioners' sugar, the perfect just-sweet-enough accent to our spiced cake. The frosting will be too soft to use right out of the food processor in step 5; be sure to chill it slightly before assembling the cake.

cakes

1 pound carrots, peeled

2 cups (8 ounces) pecans, toasted (optional)

1½ cups vegetable oil

1½ cups (10½ ounces) granulated sugar

½ cup packed (3½ ounces) light brown sugar

4 large eggs

1¼ teaspoons ground cinnamon

1¼ teaspoons baking powder

1 teaspoon baking soda

½ teaspoon ground nutmeg

½ teaspoon salt

⅛ teaspoon ground cloves

2½ cups (12½ ounces) all-purpose flour

frosting

1½ pounds cream cheese, softened

10 tablespoons unsalted butter, softened

2 tablespoons sour cream

1½ teaspoons vanilla extract

¼ teaspoon salt

2 cups (8 ounces) confectioners' sugar

1 for the cakes Adjust oven rack to middle position and heat oven to 350 degrees. Grease two 9-inch round cake pans, line with parchment paper, grease parchment, and flour pans. Working in batches, use food processor fitted with shredding disk to process carrots until shredded; set aside.

2 Fit now-empty processor with chopping blade. Pulse pecans, if using, until coarsely chopped, about 5 pulses; set aside. Process oil, granulated sugar, brown sugar, eggs, cinnamon, baking powder, baking soda, nutmeg, salt, and cloves in again-empty processor until sugars are mostly dissolved and mixture is emulsified, 10 to 12 seconds, scraping down sides of bowl as needed. Add carrots and pulse until combined, about 3 pulses. Add flour and pulse until just incorporated, about 10 pulses; do not overmix.

3 Divide batter evenly between prepared pans and smooth tops. Gently tap pans on counter to release air bubbles. Bake cakes until toothpick inserted in centers comes out with few moist crumbs attached, 35 to 40 minutes, switching and rotating pans halfway through baking.

4 Let cakes cool in pans on wire rack for 10 minutes. Remove cakes from pans, discarding parchment, and let cool completely on rack, about 2 hours.

5 for the frosting In clean, dry processor, process cream cheese, butter, sour cream, vanilla, and salt until smooth, 25 to 30 seconds, scraping down sides of bowl as needed. Add sugar and process until incorporated and frosting is creamy and glossy, about 20 seconds. Chill frosting until slightly thickened, 10 to 15 minutes.

6 Line edges of cake platter with 4 strips of parchment paper to keep platter clean. Place 1 cake layer on platter. Spread 1 cup frosting evenly over top, right to edge of cake. Top with second cake layer, press lightly to adhere, then spread remaining frosting evenly over top and sides of cake. To smooth frosting, run edge of offset spatula around cake sides and over top. If using chopped pecans, use your hand to gently press pecans onto sides of cake. Carefully remove parchment strips before serving.

PLUM-CHERRY CRISP

serves 8 to 10   **food processor size** 7 to 14 cups

why this recipe works Fruit crisps are a delicious and versatile dessert, but many versions yield gloppy, too-sweet fillings and toppings that resemble packaged granola. Depending on what fruit you choose, they can also involve quite a lot of knife work to prepare the filling. The food processor helped us prepare both the topping and the filling much more quickly so we could have this juicy, nutty dessert on the table in under an hour. First we made a perfectly crumbly, buttery crisp topping by pulsing together almonds, flour, a bit of sugar, melted butter, and oats. The oats gave the topping a nice chew, and the toasted almonds contributed deep, rich flavor that complemented the filling. For our fruit we used plums, which offered a delicate sweetness and sliced easily in the processor. We accented the plums with tart, juicy cherries, and we opted for frozen fruit to avoid the work of stemming and pitting fresh ones. A quick toss with sugar, cornstarch, lemon juice, and both vanilla and almond extracts balanced out the flavor of the filling and helped thicken the fruit juices during baking. Just 25 minutes in the oven resulted in a beautifully bubbly, golden-brown, crisp-topped dessert. There is no need to thaw the cherries for this recipe.

½ cup slivered almonds, toasted

½ cup (2½ ounces) all-purpose flour

¼ cup packed (1¾ ounces) light brown sugar

⅓ cup (2⅓ ounces) plus 2 tablespoons granulated sugar

¼ teaspoon ground cinnamon

⅛ teaspoon ground nutmeg

Salt

6 tablespoons unsalted butter, melted and cooled

½ cup old-fashioned rolled oats

1½ pounds plums, halved and pitted

1½ pounds frozen sweet cherries

2 tablespoons cornstarch

1 tablespoon lemon juice

1 teaspoon vanilla extract

¼ teaspoon almond extract

1 Adjust oven rack to lower-middle position and heat oven to 425 degrees. Process almonds, flour, brown sugar, 2 tablespoons sugar, cinnamon, nutmeg, and ⅛ teaspoon salt in food processor until finely ground, about 10 seconds. Drizzle melted butter over flour mixture and pulse until mixture resembles crumbly wet sand, about 5 pulses, scraping down sides of bowl as needed. Add oats and pulse until combined, about 3 pulses; set aside.

2 Working in batches, process plums in now-empty processor fitted with slicing disk until thinly sliced; transfer to greased 13 by 9-inch baking dish. Stir in remaining ⅓ cup sugar, cherries, cornstarch, lemon juice, vanilla, almond extract, and ½ teaspoon salt until well combined. Sprinkle evenly with almond topping, breaking up any large chunks. Bake until crisp is bubbling around edges and topping is deep golden brown, 25 to 30 minutes, rotating dish halfway through baking. Let crisp cool on wire rack for at least 20 minutes before serving.

FREE-FORM SUMMER FRUIT TART

serves 6 **food processor size** 7 to 14 cups

why this recipe works For a simple summer fruit tart that was just as appealing as harder-to-prepare pie, we started with a foolproof free-form tart dough that had a simple list of ingredients—just butter, flour, salt, and water. At first, we also included sugar, but testing revealed that not only was sweetener unnecessary, but sugar also made the crust more brittle, so we left it out. The dough was easily mixed using the food processor. To maximize the flakiness of the crust, we then employed a French pastry technique known as *fraisage*, in which the dough is smeared against the counter with the heel of your hand. This created paper-thin streaks of butter and flour that baked up into delicate, flaky layers. Satisfied with the crust, we moved on to the filling. A mix of stone fruits and berries with a little sugar to offset the fruit's tartness produced an especially nice contrast in flavors and textures. The slicing disk of the food processor efficiently cut the stone fruit thin enough that the skins could be left on without any offputting texture. As a finishing touch, we brushed the crust with water and sprinkled it with sugar to encourage browning and give it a sheen that would please both the eyes and the tastebuds.

dough

1½ cups (7½ ounces) all-purpose flour

½ teaspoon salt

10 tablespoons unsalted butter, cut into ½-inch pieces and chilled

4–6 tablespoons ice water

filling

1 pound ripe but firm peaches, nectarines, or plums, halved and pitted

5 ounces (1 cup) blackberries, blueberries, or raspberries

¼ cup (1¾ ounces) plus 1 tablespoon sugar

1 for the dough Pulse flour and salt in food processor until combined, about 5 pulses. Scatter chilled butter over top and pulse until mixture resembles coarse sand and butter pieces are size of small peas, about 10 pulses. Continue to pulse, adding water 1 tablespoon at a time, until dough begins to form small curds that hold together when pinched with your fingers, about 10 pulses.

2 Turn mixture out onto lightly floured counter and gather into rectangular pile. Starting at farthest end, use heel of your hand to smear small amount of dough against counter. Continue to smear dough until all crumbs have been worked in. Gather smeared crumbs together in another rectangular pile and repeat process.

3 Form dough into 6-inch disk, wrap tightly in plastic wrap, and refrigerate for 1 hour. Before rolling dough out, let it sit on counter to soften slightly, about 10 minutes. (Dough can be refrigerated for up to 2 days or frozen for up to 1 month. If frozen, let dough thaw completely on counter before rolling.)

4 for the filling Roll dough into 12-inch circle between 2 large sheets of parchment paper (if dough sticks to parchment, dust lightly with flour). Slide dough, still between parchment sheets, into rimmed baking sheet and refrigerate until firm, 15 to 30 minutes.

5 Adjust oven rack to middle position and heat oven to 375 degrees. Working in batches, use now-empty processor fitted with slicing disk to process peaches until thinly sliced; transfer to large bowl. Add blackberries and ¼ cup sugar and gently toss to combine.

6 Remove top sheet of parchment from dough. Mound fruit mixture in center of dough, leaving 2½-inch border around edge of fruit. Fold outermost 2 inches of dough over fruit, pleating dough every 2 to 3 inches as needed; be sure to leave ½-inch border of dough between fruit and edge of tart. Gently pinch pleated dough to secure, but do not press dough into fruit.

7 Brush top and sides of dough with water and sprinkle with remaining 1 tablespoon sugar. Bake until crust is golden brown and fruit is bubbling, about 1 hour, rotating sheet halfway through baking.

8 Let tart cool in sheet for 10 minutes. Use parchment to transfer tart to wire rack, then discard parchment. Let tart cool until juices have thickened, about 25 minutes. Serve slightly warm or at room temperature.

CLASSIC APPLE PIE

serves 8   food processor size 7 to 14 cups

why this recipe works Just because apple pie is classic, that doesn't mean it's easy, but our food processor version is as simple as it gets. For pie dough that mixed and rolled out easily, we added sour cream, which helped keep it tender. Our filling combined two varieties of apples for a mix of sweet-tart flavors and soft-firm textures. With help from the food processor, we sliced over 3 pounds of apples in no time. Microwaving the sliced apples before assembling the pie let them shrink just enough to prevent a gap from forming under the top crust during baking. Starting the pie in a 425-degree oven helped the crust develop good color. We then allowed the pie to gently finish baking at a lower temperature. You will need a 9-inch deep-dish pie plate for this recipe.

dough

⅓ cup ice water, plus extra as needed

3 tablespoons sour cream

2½ cups (12½ ounces) all-purpose flour

1 tablespoon granulated sugar

1 teaspoon salt

16 tablespoons unsalted butter, cut into ¼-inch pieces and frozen for 10 to 15 minutes

filling

2 pounds Golden Delicious, Fuji, or Jonagold apples, peeled, cored, and halved

1½ pounds Granny Smith, Cortland, or Empire apples, peeled, cored, and halved

6 tablespoons (2⅔ ounces) plus 1 teaspoon granulated sugar

2 tablespoons packed brown sugar

2 tablespoons all-purpose flour

1 teaspoon grated lemon zest plus 1 tablespoon juice

¼ teaspoon salt

⅛ teaspoon ground cinnamon

1 large egg white, lightly beaten

1 for the dough Whisk ice water and sour cream together in bowl. Pulse flour, sugar, and salt in food processor until combined, about 5 pulses. Scatter frozen butter over top and pulse mixture until butter is size of large peas, about 10 pulses.

2 Pour half of sour cream mixture over flour mixture and pulse until incorporated, about 3 pulses. Repeat with remaining sour cream mixture. Pinch dough with your fingers; if dough feels dry and does not hold together, sprinkle 1 to 2 tablespoons more ice water over mixture and pulse until dough forms large clumps and no dry flour remains, 3 to 5 pulses.

3 Divide dough into 2 equal pieces. Turn each piece of dough out onto sheet of plastic wrap and flatten into 4-inch disk. Wrap each piece tightly and refrigerate for 1 hour. Before rolling dough out, let it sit on counter to soften slightly,

about 10 minutes. (Dough can be refrigerated for up to 2 days or frozen for up to 1 month. If frozen, let dough thaw completely on counter before rolling it out.)

4 Roll 1 piece of dough between 2 large sheets of parchment paper to 12-inch circle. (If dough is soft and/or sticky, refrigerate until firm.) Remove parchment on top of dough round and flip dough into 9-inch deep-dish pie plate; peel off second layer of parchment. Lift dough and gently press it into pie plate, letting excess hang over plate's edge. Cover loosely with plastic and refrigerate until firm, about 30 minutes. Roll second piece of dough between 2 large sheets of parchment paper to 12-inch circle. Slide dough, still between parchment sheets, into rimmed baking sheet and refrigerate for 30 minutes.

5 for the filling Adjust oven rack to lowest position and heat oven to 425 degrees. Line rimmed baking sheet with aluminum foil. Working in batches, use now-empty processor fitted

with slicing disk to process apples until thinly sliced; transfer to large bowl. Add 6 tablespoons granulated sugar, brown sugar, flour, lemon zest, salt, and cinnamon and gently toss to combine. Microwave apple mixture, stirring occasionally, until apples are slightly pliable, about 3 minutes. Let apple mixture cool slightly, about 5 minutes, then stir in lemon juice. Spread apple mixture in chilled dough-lined pie plate, mounding apples slightly in middle.

6 Loosely roll top dough round around rolling pin, then gently unroll it over filling. Trim overhanging dough ½ inch beyond lip of pie plate. Pinch edges of top and bottom crusts firmly together. Tuck overhang under itself; folded edge should be flush with edge of pie plate. Crimp dough evenly around edge of pie using your fingers. Cut four 2-inch slits in top of dough. Brush surface with beaten egg white and sprinkle evenly with remaining 1 teaspoon granulated sugar.

7 Place pie in prepared sheet and bake until crust is light golden brown, about 25 minutes. Reduce oven temperature to 375 degrees, rotate sheet, and continue to bake until juice is bubbling and crust is deep golden brown, 30 to 35 minutes. Let pie cool on wire rack until filling has set, about 2 hours. Serve slightly warm or at room temperature.

CHOCOLATE CHIP COOKIES

makes 16 large cookies   **food processor size** 7 to 14 cups

why this recipe works Our refined version of the classic chocolate chip cookie is a harmonious blend of rich toffee notes and a just-right amount of chocolate chips, with a crisp edge and a chewy interior. To avoid all the strenuous hand stirring typically required for a well-mixed cookie dough, we turned to the food processor. All it took was a few tweaks to the ingredient order to get perfect cookie dough without ever having to pick up a mixing spoon. Most cookie doughs are made by first creaming together softened butter and sugar. We found that browning the butter on the stovetop lent the perfect chewy texture and complex, nutty flavor. We then incorporated the sugar, vanilla, baking soda, and eggs (one whole egg plus an extra yolk for richness). This is when one of our food processor adaptations came into play; instead of waiting to add the leavener with the rest of the dry ingredients, we added the baking soda early to allow it enough time to become fully incorporated and activated in the dough. We also found that the cookie dough worked best in the food processor if we added our mix-ins (chocolate chips and nuts) prior to the flour rather than all the way at the end. When we added the flour first, the dough tended to get overworked and produced a tougher, cakier cookie. Once we made these small adjustments, we had a bowl-free chocolate chip cookie recipe that left back-of-the-bag recipes in the dust. The recipe will work with light brown sugar, but the cookies will not be as richly flavored.

14 tablespoons unsalted butter

½ cup (3½ ounces) granulated sugar

¾ cup packed (5¼ ounces) dark brown sugar

1 large egg plus 1 large yolk

1 teaspoon vanilla extract

1 teaspoon salt

½ teaspoon baking soda

1¼ cups (7½ ounces) semisweet chocolate chips

¾ cup pecans or walnuts, toasted (optional)

1¾ cups (8¾ ounces) all-purpose flour

1 Adjust oven rack to middle position and heat oven to 375 degrees. Line 2 baking sheets with parchment paper. Heat 10 tablespoons butter in 10-inch skillet over medium-high heat. Cook, swirling pan constantly, until butter is dark golden brown and has nutty aroma, 1 to 3 minutes. Off heat, swirl in remaining 4 tablespoons butter until melted. Transfer browned butter to food processor and let cool for 15 minutes.

2 Add granulated sugar, brown sugar, egg and yolk, vanilla, salt, and baking soda to processor and process until combined and mixture is smooth, about 6 seconds, scraping down sides of bowl as needed. Let mixture sit for 3 minutes, then process for additional 5 seconds. Repeat process of sitting and processing 2 more times until mixture is thick, smooth, and shiny.

3 Add chocolate chips and pecans, if using, and pulse until incorporated, about 2 pulses. Add flour and pulse until just incorporated, about 8 pulses; do not overmix.

4 Working with 3 tablespoons dough at a time, roll into balls and space 2 inches apart on prepared sheets. (Raw cookies can be frozen for up to 1 month; bake frozen cookies in 300-degree oven for 30 to 35 minutes.)

5 Bake cookies, 1 sheet at a time, until golden brown and edges have begun to set but centers are still soft and puffy, 10 to 14 minutes, rotating sheet halfway through baking. Let cookies cool on sheet for 5 minutes, then transfer to wire rack and let cool completely before serving.

CHEWY SUGAR COOKIES

makes 24 cookies   **food processor size** 7 to 14 cups

why this recipe works Traditional recipes for sugar cookies require a great deal of attention to detail. The butter must be at precisely the right temperature, and slight variations in measures can result in cookies that spread too much or become brittle and hard upon cooling. The keys to the foolproof sugar cookies of our dreams turned out to be the right mix of fats, a simple but precise food-processor mixing method, and a surprise secret ingredient—cream cheese. A ratio of approximately 1 part saturated fat (melted butter) to 3 parts unsaturated fat (vegetable oil) gave us optimal chew. The food processor brought the dough together quickly and completely, which helped prevent overmixing. We first processed our wet ingredients, including a small amount of cream cheese for richness, and our leaveners—both the traditional baking powder and also baking soda, which reacted with the acidic cream cheese to give us a beautiful crackly top. Finally we mixed in the flour, pulsing just enough to eliminate any visible streaks. The last step was rolling the cookies in sugar before baking for a sweet, crisp crust. For simple variations we added chai spices to one batch and lime zest and coconut flakes to another. The final dough will be slightly softer than most cookie doughs. For the best results, handle the dough as briefly and gently as possible when shaping the cookies. Overworking the dough will result in flatter cookies.

1½ cups (10½ ounces) sugar, plus ⅓ cup for rolling

6 tablespoons unsalted butter, softened

⅓ cup vegetable oil

2 ounces cream cheese, softened

1 large egg

1 tablespoon whole milk

2 teaspoons vanilla extract

1 teaspoon baking powder

½ teaspoon baking soda

½ teaspoon salt

2¼ cups (11¼ ounces) all-purpose flour

1 Adjust oven rack to middle position and heat oven to 350 degrees. Line 2 rimmed baking sheets with parchment paper. Pulse 1½ cups sugar, butter, oil, cream cheese, egg, milk, vanilla, baking powder, baking soda, and salt in food processor until just combined, 5 to 7 pulses, scraping down sides of bowl as needed (some small lumps of butter and cream cheese will remain but will smooth out later). Add flour and pulse until just incorporated, 10 to 12 pulses, scraping down sides of bowl halfway through pulsing; do not overmix.

2 Turn dough out onto counter and divide into 24 equal pieces, about 2 tablespoons each. Using hands, roll dough into balls. Working in batches, roll balls in reserved ⅓ cup sugar to coat and space evenly in prepared sheets, 12 dough balls per sheet. Using bottom of drinking glass, flatten dough balls until 2 inches in diameter. Sprinkle tops evenly with 4 teaspoons sugar remaining in shallow dish (2 teaspoons per sheet), discarding remaining sugar.

3 Bake cookies, 1 sheet at a time, until edges are set and beginning to brown, 11 to 13 minutes, rotating sheet halfway through baking. Let cookies cool in sheet for 5 minutes, then transfer to wire rack and let cool completely before serving.

CHEWY CHAI-SPICE COOKIES

Add ¼ teaspoon ground cinnamon, ¼ teaspoon ground ginger, ¼ teaspoon ground cardamom, ¼ teaspoon ground cloves, and pinch pepper to processor with sugar. Reduce vanilla to 1 teaspoon.

CHEWY COCONUT-LIME COOKIES

Add ½ cup sweetened shredded coconut and 1 teaspoon grated lime zest to processor with sugar. Substitute 1 tablespoon lime juice for vanilla extract.

ALMOND BISCOTTI

makes 30 cookies   food processor size 7 to 14 cups

why this recipe works Our ideal biscotti is somewhere between the dry, hard Italian original and the buttery, tender American version. We wanted nut-filled cookies that were crisp enough for dunking, yet not tooth-shattering. Knowing that the texture depended, in part, on the amount of butter, we reduced the amount we used so it was just enough to give us cookies with a good crunch. However, we then didn't have enough butter to effectively cream with the sugar, so we needed to find another way to aerate the dough. Whipping the eggs in the food processor until they were light in color and then adding the sugar did the trick. To moderate the crunchiness, we ground some of the lightly toasted nuts in the processor and substituted them for a portion of the flour. With less flour, less gluten formed, so the biscotti were more tender—and they had nutty flavor in every bite. We baked the dough in two neat rectangles, then sliced them and baked the slices on a wire rack set in a baking sheet, flipping them halfway through baking. The rack allowed air circulation around the cookies, making them evenly crisp. Be sure to toast the almonds just until fragrant; they will continue to toast while the biscotti bake.

1¼ cups whole almonds, lightly toasted

1¾ cups (8¾ ounces) all-purpose flour

2 teaspoons baking powder

¼ teaspoon salt

2 large eggs, plus 1 large white beaten with pinch salt

1 cup (7 ounces) sugar

4 tablespoons unsalted butter, melted and cooled

1½ teaspoons almond extract

½ teaspoon vanilla extract

1 Adjust oven rack to middle position and heat oven to 325 degrees. Using ruler and pencil, draw two 8 by 3-inch rectangles, spaced 4 inches apart, on piece of parchment paper. Grease baking sheet and place parchment on it, pencil side down.

2 Pulse 1 cup almonds in food processor until coarsely chopped, 8 to 10 pulses; set aside. Process remaining ¼ cup almonds in now-empty processor until finely ground, about 45 seconds. Add flour, baking powder, and salt and pulse until combined, about 5 pulses; set aside.

3 Process 2 eggs in again-empty processor until lightened in color and almost doubled in volume, about 3 minutes. With processor running, slowly add sugar and process until thoroughly combined, about 15 seconds. Add melted butter, almond extract, and vanilla and process until combined, about 10 seconds, scraping down sides of bowl as needed. Add half

of flour mixture and pulse until just combined, about 5 pulses. Add remaining flour mixture and chopped almonds and pulse until just combined, about 5 pulses; do not overmix.

4 Divide batter in half. With floured hands, form each half into 8 by 3-inch rectangle, using lines on parchment as guide. Spray each loaf lightly with vegetable oil spray. Using greased rubber spatula, smooth tops and sides of rectangles. Gently brush tops of loaves with egg white wash. Bake loaves until golden and just beginning to crack on top, 25 to 30 minutes, rotating sheet halfway through baking.

5 Let loaves cool on sheet for 30 minutes. Transfer loaves to cutting board. Using serrated knife, slice each loaf on slight bias into ½-inch-thick slices. Space slices, with 1 cut side down, about ¼ inch apart on wire rack set in rimmed baking sheet. Bake until crisp and golden brown on both sides, about 35 minutes, flipping slices halfway through baking. Let cool completely before serving.

CHEWY BROWNIES

makes 24 brownies   food processor size 7 to 14 cups

why this recipe works For the ultimate chewy brownies, we had to find the right balance of butter, oil, and eggs along with the perfect blend of chocolate and cocoa powder to achieve a rich, complex flavor without greasiness. For well-balanced chocolate flavor, we started with a base of Dutch-processed cocoa to provide a strong backbone, plus unsweetened chocolate for pure, intense flavor and a tiny bit of espresso powder to boost the intensity of the chocolate. The addition of 2 egg yolks along with 2 whole eggs helped to bind some of the fat in the brownies, combating greasiness; and adding bittersweet chocolate chunks last ensured that we would get nice pockets of gooey, melted chocolate evenly dispersed throughout the brownies. Using the food processor, we could make the batter in under a minute without any hand stirring, and the batter went straight from the bowl of the processor to the pan to the oven. For the chewiest texture, it is important to let the brownies cool thoroughly before cutting. If your baking dish is glass, cool the brownies for 10 minutes, then remove them promptly from the dish (the superior heat retention of glass can lead to overbaking). For best results, boil a small pot of water and then measure out the amount called for in the recipe, rather than boiling the measured amount of water, since some will be lost to evaporation.

½ cup plus 2 tablespoons vegetable oil

½ cup plus 2 tablespoons boiling water

⅓ cup (1 ounce) Dutch processed cocoa powder

4 tablespoons unsalted butter, softened

1½ teaspoons instant espresso powder (optional)

2 ounces unsweetened chocolate, broken into ½-inch pieces

2 teaspoons vanilla extract

¾ teaspoon salt

2½ cups (17½ ounces) sugar

2 large eggs, plus 2 large yolks

1¾ cups (8¾ ounces) all-purpose flour

6 ounces bittersweet chocolate, broken into ½-inch pieces

1 Adjust oven rack to lowest position and heat oven to 350 degrees. Make foil sling for 13 by 9-inch baking pan by folding 2 long sheets of aluminum foil; first sheet should be 13 inches wide and second sheet should be 9 inches wide. Lay sheets of foil in pan perpendicular to each other, with extra foil hanging over edges of pan. Push foil into corners and up sides of pan, smoothing foil flush to pan. Grease foil.

2 Process oil, boiling water, cocoa, butter, espresso powder, if using, unsweetened chocolate, vanilla, and salt in food processor until chocolate is melted and mixture is smooth, 10 to 12 seconds, scraping down sides of bowl as needed. Add sugar and eggs and yolks and process until combined, about 5 seconds. Add flour and bittersweet chocolate and pulse until just incorporated, about 5 pulses; do not overmix.

3 Transfer batter to prepared pan and smooth top. Bake until toothpick inserted halfway between edge and center comes out with few moist crumbs attached, 30 to 35 minutes, rotating pan halfway through baking.

4 Let brownies cool in pan on wire rack for 1½ hours. Using foil overhang, lift brownies from pan and return to wire rack. Let cool completely, about 1 hour. Cut into 2-inch squares and serve.

NUTELLA HAZELNUT TRUFFLES

makes 24 truffles   **food processor size** 7 to 14 cups

why this recipe works Most truffles are nothing more than a ganache that's been chilled and rolled into balls. These are different. We used hazelnut spread (Nutella), ground hazelnuts, and whole hazelnuts to pack our truffles with maximum hazelnut flavor (without turning to flavored extract or booze). We started by processing the Nutella with melted butter, sugar, and some milk. Cocoa powder added to the mixture heightened the Nutella's mellow milk chocolate flavor. Pulsing in cornflakes helped bind the mixture together and gave the truffles a subtle crunch. We then spread this mixture in a pan, chilled it, and sliced it into squares, and each square got wrapped around a whole hazelnut. A coating of ground hazelnuts gave the truffles the distinctive, slightly sweet and rich flavor we were looking for. The texture of the truffles is best when they are served chilled. Whole almonds can be substituted for the hazelnuts, if desired.

½ cup hazelnuts, toasted and skinned, plus 24 hazelnuts, toasted and skinned, for truffle centers

¾ cup Nutella

½ cup (3½ ounces) sugar

¼ cup whole milk

3 tablespoons unsalted butter, softened

1 tablespoon unsweetened cocoa powder

2 cups cornflakes

1 Make foil sling for 13 by 9-inch baking pan by folding 2 long sheets of aluminum foil; first sheet should be 13 inches wide and second sheet should be 9 inches wide. Lay sheets of foil in pan perpendicular to each other, with extra foil hanging over edges of pan. Push foil into corners and up sides of pan, smoothing foil flush to pan. Grease foil.

2 Process ½ cup hazelnuts in food processor until finely ground, about 15 seconds; transfer to shallow dish and set aside. Process Nutella, sugar, milk, butter, and cocoa in now-empty processor until combined and mixture is smooth, about 10 seconds, scraping down sides of bowl as needed.

Add cornflakes and pulse until coarsely ground and mixture is combined, about 10 pulses. Scrape mixture into prepared pan and press firmly into even layer with greased spatula. Refrigerate until firm, about 10 minutes.

3 Using foil overhang, lift Nutella mixture from pan and transfer to cutting board; discard foil. Cut Nutella mixture into 24 squares, then mold each around whole hazelnut to encase completely. Roll truffles in ground nuts to coat and transfer to platter. Cover and refrigerate for at least 2 hours or up to 1 week. Let truffles sit at room temperature for 5 to 10 minutes before serving.

CHILL OUT WITH ELEGANT CREAMY DESSERTS

Frozen and chilled desserts have a reputation for being finicky; you usually need a load of specialized equipment to even attempt them at home. An ice cream maker is a great tool, but if you don't plan to whip up ice cream on a regular basis, it's probably not worth the expense (or the counter space). However, just because you don't have one, that doesn't mean you can't have homemade ice cream whenever you want; just use your all-star multitasking food processor. Plus, its powers of whipping and mixing can also tackle tricky chilled desserts like mousse and cream pie. And it handles both the crust and the filling of tricky dishes like cheesecake.

FOOD PROCESSOR FINDINGS

Here are a few tricks we've discovered for making chilled and frozen desserts at home with your food processor:

1 The food processor is an ideal tool for making the smoothest, creamiest custards ever for recipes like Icebox Chocolate Cream Pie (page 162) and the filling of our Classic Cheesecake (page 158). Its quick, efficient mixing actually creates fewer air bubbles in the mixtures than a stand mixer would.

2 To make the creamiest frozen desserts in the processor and avoid iciness, we freeze the base for frozen desserts like ice cream in ice cube trays before processing it. Freezing in these smaller amounts speeds things up and helps encourage the formation of smaller, less noticeable ice crystals that our tongues can't detect, which makes the ice cream feel smoother and taste creamier.

3 Using the food processor is a great way to whip cream, either as part of a recipe or to top a dessert. It works best if you use at least 1½ cups of cream; any less liquid and there won't be enough volume to effectively whip in a large processor bowl.

UNUSUAL TOOL, CLASSIC RESULTS

Traditional ice cream makers work through a combination of cooling and constant-yet-gentle churning that turns a loose dairy or fruit base into a semisoft consistency. The churning incorporates a small amount of air that is crucial to a creamy final product. We get the same rich, ultrapremium texture in our food processor ice cream by using sweetened condensed milk and melted white chocolate for structure. We also freeze our ice cream base in ice cube trays to minimize the ice crystals. Pureeing the cubes in the food processor incorporates just enough air for supercreamy results.

ultra-creamy, dense texture of our favorite supermarket vanilla ice cream, Ben & Jerry's Vanilla

super-premium texture of our Easiest-Ever Vanilla Ice Cream

CLASSIC CHEESECAKE

serves 12 to 16   food processor size 11 to 14 cups

why this recipe works Cheesecake can be a notoriously fussy endeavor, often involving messing with a water bath, but not this recipe. For starters, both the crust and the filling come together in the food processor, helping to make the process fast and easy. After assembling and prebaking a simple graham cracker crust, we made our filling. The processor's blade deftly cut the cream cheese (along with eggs, sugar, heavy cream, vanilla, and sour cream for a little extra tang) into a thoroughly smooth batter and actually produced fewer pesky air bubbles than a stand mixer. By baking at a very low temperature, we could ditch the water bath and still obtain a smooth, crack-free top. Reduce the oven temperature as soon as the crust is finished baking and be sure it has dropped to 250 degrees before you begin baking the cheesecake. Thoroughly scrape down the sides and bottom of the processor bowl as you make the filling to eliminate lumps.

crust

6 whole graham crackers, broken into 1-inch pieces

⅓ cup (2⅓ ounces) sugar

½ cup (2½ ounces) all-purpose flour

¼ teaspoon salt

6 tablespoons unsalted butter, melted

filling

2 pounds cream cheese

1¼ cups (8¾ ounces) sugar

4 large eggs

¼ cup heavy cream

¼ cup sour cream

2 teaspoons vanilla extract

1 for the crust Adjust oven rack to middle position and heat oven to 325 degrees. Process cracker pieces and sugar in food processor until finely ground, about 30 seconds. Add flour and salt and pulse to combine, about 2 pulses. Add butter and pulse until crumbs are evenly moistened, about 10 pulses.

2 Grease bottom and sides of 9-inch springform pan. Using your hands, press crumb mixture evenly into pan bottom. Using bottom of measuring cup, firmly pack crust into pan. Bake crust until fragrant and beginning to brown around edges, about 13 minutes. Let crust cool completely on wire rack, about 30 minutes. Reduce oven temperature to 250 degrees.

3 for the filling Process cream cheese and sugar in clean, dry processor until smooth, about 3 minutes, scraping down sides of bowl as needed. With processor running, add eggs, 1 at a time, until just incorporated, about 30 seconds. Scrape down sides of bowl. Add cream, sour cream, and vanilla and process until combined, about 30 seconds.

4 Pour cheesecake mixture into cooled crust. Gently tap pan on counter to release air bubbles. Gently draw tines of fork across surface of cake to pop air bubbles that have risen to surface.

5 Once oven temperature has reduced to 250 degrees, bake cheesecake until edges are set and center jiggles slightly when shaken and registers 155 degrees, 80 to 90 minutes. Transfer cheesecake to wire rack and let cool to room temperature, about 2 hours. Refrigerate cheesecake, uncovered, until cold, about 6 hours. (Cake can be covered and refrigerated for up to 4 days.)

6 To unmold cheesecake, run tip of sharp paring knife between cake and sides of pan and remove sides of pan. Slide thin metal spatula between crust and pan bottom to loosen, and slide cake onto serving platter. Let cheesecake sit at room temperature for 30 minutes. Using warm, dry knife, cut into wedges and serve.

ICEBOX KEY LIME PIE

serves 8 **food processor size** 11 to 14 cups

why this recipe works Traditional Key lime pie recipes call for stirring sweetened condensed milk, raw egg yolks, and lime juice together and pouring that mixture into a prebaked graham cracker crust. The acid in the lime juice "cooks" the protein in the milk and yolks, creating a custardy, firm filling. For a take on this classic pie that didn't rely on raw egg yolks, we used a combination of instant vanilla pudding, gelatin, and cream cheese whipped together in the food processor with the usual lime juice and condensed milk to thicken our no-cook pie's filling to a perfect, smooth consistency. A full cup of fresh lime juice produced a pie with bracing lime flavor. Lime zest added another layer of flavor, and processing the zest with a little sugar offset its sourness and eliminated the annoying chewy bits. We found only minor differences in taste when we used conventional Persian limes rather than real Key limes, but feel free to use Key limes, if desired; you will need about 40 Key limes to yield 1 cup of juice. Serve with whipped cream (see page 11).

crust

8 whole graham crackers, broken into 1-inch pieces

1 tablespoon sugar

5 tablespoons unsalted butter, melted

filling

1¼ teaspoons unflavored gelatin

1 tablespoon grated lime zest plus 1 cup juice (8 limes)

¼ cup (1¾ ounces) sugar

8 ounces cream cheese, softened

1 (14-ounce) can sweetened condensed milk

⅓ cup instant vanilla pudding mix

1 teaspoon vanilla extract

1 for the crust Adjust oven rack to middle position and heat oven to 325 degrees. Process cracker pieces and sugar in food processor until finely ground, about 30 seconds. Add butter and pulse until crumbs are evenly moistened, about 10 pulses.

2 Sprinkle mixture into 9-inch pie plate. Using bottom of measuring cup, firmly pack crust into even layer on bottom and sides of pie plate. Bake crust until fragrant and set, about 20 minutes, rotating pie plate halfway through baking. Let crust cool completely on wire rack, about 30 minutes.

3 for the filling Sprinkle gelatin over ¼ cup lime juice in bowl and let sit until gelatin softens, about 5 minutes. Microwave mixture until bubbling around edges and gelatin dissolves, about 30 seconds.

4 Process sugar and lime zest in food processor until sugar turns bright green, about 30 seconds. Add cream cheese, condensed milk, pudding mix, vanilla, and gelatin mixture and process until combined and smooth, about 30 seconds, scraping down sides of bowl as needed. With processor running, slowly add remaining ¾ cup lime juice until incorporated, about 30 seconds.

5 Pour filling into cooled crust and smooth top. Press plastic wrap directly on surface of filling and refrigerate pie until filling is chilled and set, at least 3 hours or up to 24 hours. Using warm, dry knife, cut into slices and serve.

ICEBOX CHOCOLATE CREAM PIE

serves 8   food processor size 11 to 14 cups

why this recipe works Chocolate cream pies usually look superb, but they're often gluey, overly sweet, and impossible to slice. We wanted a sweet, creamy filling that fell somewhere between a pudding and a mousse, and we wanted the recipe to be simple and foolproof. A no-cook method using gelatin instead of the usual eggs and cornstarch eliminated the need for any stovetop work. Blooming the gelatin in milk and cream and then heating it briefly in the microwave created just the texture we were after. We played with varying amounts of milk and cream; too much cream made the pie bland; too little, and it tasted watery. We settled on a 3:1 ratio for the best creaminess. A combination of bittersweet chocolate and cocoa powder gave us the best chocolate flavor and texture. The food processor helped us make a perfectly silky-smooth mixture that set up into the chocolate filling of our dreams. Oreo cookies (cream and all) ground in the processor and mixed with a little melted butter made the tastiest, most tender, sliceable crumb crust. We then had only to make a quick food processor whipped cream for the top. Other brands of chocolate sandwich cookies may be substituted, but avoid "double-filled" cookies because the proportion of cookie to filling won't be correct.

crust

16 Oreo cookies, broken into rough pieces

4 tablespoons unsalted butter, melted

filling

1½ cups heavy cream

½ cup whole milk

½ teaspoon vanilla extract

1¾ teaspoons unflavored gelatin

2 ounces bittersweet chocolate, coarsely chopped

3 tablespoons sugar

2 tablespoons unsweetened cocoa powder

⅛ teaspoon salt

whipped cream

1½ cups heavy cream, chilled

2 tablespoons sugar

½ teaspoon vanilla extract

1 for the crust Adjust oven rack to middle position and heat oven to 325 degrees. Process cookie pieces in food processor until finely ground, about 30 seconds. Add butter and pulse until crumbs are evenly moistened, about 10 pulses.

2 Sprinkle mixture into 9-inch pie plate. Using bottom of measuring cup, firmly pack crust into even layer on bottom and sides of pie plate. Bake crust until fragrant and set, 13 to 18 minutes, rotating pie plate halfway through baking. Let crust cool completely on wire rack, about 30 minutes.

3 for the filling Combine cream, milk, and vanilla in 2-cup liquid measuring cup. Sprinkle gelatin over top and let sit until gelatin softens, about 5 minutes. Microwave cream mixture, stirring occasionally, until hot but not boiling and gelatin is completely dissolved, about 2 minutes.

4 Add chocolate, sugar, cocoa, and salt to clean, dry processor. With processor running, slowly add hot cream mixture and process until chocolate is melted and filling is smooth, about 1 minute, scraping down sides of bowl as needed. Pour filling into cooled crust and smooth top. Press plastic wrap directly on surface of filling and refrigerate pie until filling is chilled and set, at least 3 hours or up to 24 hours.

5 for the whipped cream Before serving, process cream, sugar, and vanilla in clean, dry processor to soft peaks, about 1 minute, scraping down sides of bowl as needed. Spread whipped cream attractively over top of pie. Using warm, dry knife, cut into slices and serve.

SUMMER BERRY PIE

serves 8   **food processor size** 7 to 14 cups

why this recipe works A fresh berry pie might seem like an easy-to-pull-off summer dessert, but most of the recipes we tried buried the berries in gluey thickeners or embedded them in bouncy gelatin. Our goal was to make a pie with great texture and flavor—and still keep it simple. We started by throwing together our simple graham cracker crust. It had the perfect crisp texture and not-too-sweet flavor to offset the juicy berries. For the filling, we used a combination of raspberries, blackberries, and blueberries. After trying a few different methods, we found a solution that both bound the berries in the graham cracker crust and intensified their bright flavor: We processed a portion of the berries in the food processor until they made a smooth puree, which we then thickened with cornstarch. To finish our pie, we tossed the remaining berries with warm jelly for a glossy coat and a shot of sweetness. Pressed gently into the puree, the berries stayed put and tasted great. Feel free to vary the amount of each berry as desired as long as you have 6 cups of berries total; do not substitute frozen berries here. Serve with whipped cream (see page 11).

crust

8 whole graham crackers, broken into 1-inch pieces

1 tablespoon sugar

5 tablespoons unsalted butter, melted

filling

10 ounces (2 cups) raspberries

10 ounces (2 cups) blackberries

10 ounces (2 cups) blueberries

½ cup (3½ ounces) sugar

3 tablespoons cornstarch

⅛ teaspoon salt

1 tablespoon lemon juice

2 tablespoons red currant or apple jelly

1 for the crust Adjust oven rack to middle position and heat oven to 325 degrees. Process cracker pieces and sugar in food processor until finely ground, about 30 seconds. Add butter and pulse until crumbs are evenly moistened, about 10 pulses.

2 Sprinkle mixture into 9-inch pie plate. Using bottom of measuring cup, firmly pack crust into even layer on bottom and sides of pie plate. Bake crust until fragrant and set, about 20 minutes, rotating pie plate halfway through baking. Let crust cool completely on wire rack, about 30 minutes.

3 for the filling Gently toss berries together in large bowl. Process 2½ cups berries in food processor until very smooth, about 1 minute. Strain puree through fine-mesh strainer into small saucepan, pressing on solids to extract as much puree as possible (you should have about 1½ cups); discard solids.

4 Whisk sugar, cornstarch, and salt together in bowl, then whisk into strained puree. Bring puree mixture to boil over medium heat and cook, stirring constantly, until thickened to puddinglike consistency, about 7 minutes. Off heat, stir in lemon juice and let cool slightly.

5 Pour warm berry puree into cooled crust. Microwave jelly in bowl until melted, about 30 seconds, then pour over remaining berries and toss to coat. Spread berries evenly over puree and lightly press them into puree. Cover pie loosely with plastic wrap and refrigerate until filling is chilled and set, at least 3 hours or up to 24 hours. Using warm, dry knife, cut into slices and serve.

FRESH STRAWBERRY MOUSSE

serves 4 to 6 **food processor size** 7 to 14 cups

why this recipe works There's a good reason that strawberry mousse recipes aren't very prevalent: The berries contain lots of juice, and that can ruin the texture of a delicate mousse, which should be creamy and rich. Plus, the fruit flavor produced by most strawberry mousse recipes is too subtle. To tackle these challenges and create a truly bright, flavorful strawberry mousse, we started by processing berries into small pieces and macerating them with sugar and a little salt. This caused them to release their liquid, which we then reduced to a syrup before adding it to the mousse—a technique that not only limited the amount of moisture in the dessert but also concentrated the berry flavor. Then we fully pureed the juiced berries, which contributed bright, fresh berry flavor. Finally, we chose our stabilizers carefully: gelatin for structure and cream cheese, an unusual addition, for richer, creamier body. The whole thing whipped up to a perfectly smooth mousse right in the food processor. For more complex berry flavor, replace the 3 tablespoons of strawberry juice in step 2 with strawberry or raspberry liqueur.

2 pounds strawberries, hulled (6½ cups)

½ cup (3½ ounces) sugar

Pinch salt

1¾ teaspoons unflavored gelatin

¾ cup heavy cream, chilled

4 ounces cream cheese, softened

1 Cut enough strawberries into ¼-inch pieces to measure 1 cup; refrigerate until ready to serve. Working in 2 batches, pulse remaining strawberries in food processor until most pieces measure ¼ to ½ inch (some larger pieces are fine), 6 to 10 pulses; transfer to bowl. Stir in ¼ cup sugar and salt and let sit for 45 minutes, stirring occasionally.

2 Strain processed strawberries through fine-mesh strainer into bowl; set strawberries aside. Measure 3 tablespoons drained juice into small bowl, sprinkle gelatin over top, and let sit until gelatin softens, about 5 minutes. Pour remaining drained juice into small saucepan and cook over medium-high heat until reduced to 3 tablespoons, about 10 minutes. Off heat, stir in softened gelatin mixture until dissolved.

3 Return drained strawberries to now-empty processor and process until very smooth, about 30 seconds. Strain puree through fine-mesh strainer into bowl, pressing on solids to extract as much puree as possible (you should have about 1⅔ cups puree); discard solids.

4 Process heavy cream and remaining ¼ cup sugar in again-empty processor to stiff peaks, about 1 minute, scraping down sides of bowl as needed. Add cream cheese, strawberry puree, and gelatin mixture and process until combined and smooth, about 30 seconds.

5 Portion mousse evenly into dessert dishes and chill for at least 4 hours or up to 2 days. (If chilled longer than 6 hours, let mousse sit at room temperature for 15 minutes before serving.) Garnish with reserved diced strawberries and serve.

ALL-SEASON STRAWBERRY MOUSSE
Substitute 1½ pounds (5¼ cups) thawed frozen strawberries for fresh strawberries. Omit strawberry garnish and skip processing berries in step 1. Let frozen berries thaw completely in colander set over bowl to catch juice, and use 3 table-spoons juice in step 2. Add all of sugar and salt to processor with cream.

LEMON ICE

serves 8   **food processor size** 7 to 14 cups

why this recipe works Frozen ices are a quick and easy dessert, but with so few ingredients they have a tendency to be plagued by harsh and unbalanced flavors. We wanted a lemon ice that struck a perfect sweet-tart balance without any trace of bitterness. A single cup of sugar gave our lemon ice the ideal amount of sweetness; less sugar left it with a pronounced bitterness, and more sugar made our ice taste like frozen lemonade concentrate. We added a bit of vodka to ensure a soft, slightly slushy texture; the alcohol lowers the freezing temperature of the mixture and helps keep it creamy. A pinch of salt gave the flavor a boost. To achieve an ice with a fluffy, coarse-grained texture and crystalline crunch, we froze the mixture in ice cube trays and then pulsed the cubes in the food processor. This simple method adapted beautifully to other citrus ices for lemon-lime and orange variations. The texture of this dessert is also improved by placing the serving bowls in the freezer until the ice is ready to serve. You will need two standard 16-cube ice cube trays for this recipe. We recommend making this recipe with bottled water; tasters preferred lemon ice made with spring or mineral water. The processed ice is best served within an hour of being ready; it does not store well in the freezer.

2¼ cups water

1 cup lemon juice (6 lemons)

1 cup (7 ounces) sugar

2 tablespoons vodka (optional)

⅛ teaspoon salt

1 Whisk all ingredients together in 4-cup liquid measuring cup until sugar has dissolved. Divide mixture evenly between 2 ice cube trays and freeze until solid, at least 3 hours or up to 5 days.

2 Freeze glass bowl until chilled. Working in 4 batches, process cubes in food processor until smooth and no large lumps remain, about 30 seconds, scraping down sides of bowl as needed; transfer mixture to chilled bowl and freeze while processing remaining cubes. Scoop ice into chilled dessert dishes and serve immediately.

LEMON-LIME ICE

Substitute ½ cup lime juice for half of lemon juice and tequila for vodka.

ORANGE ICE

Reduce lemon juice to 2 tablespoons and sugar to ¾ cup. Add ¾ cup orange juice to ice mixture in step 1.

EASIEST-EVER VANILLA ICE CREAM

makes about 1 quart **food processor size** 7 to 14 cups

why this recipe works Making your own ice cream is a fun and delicious project, but it has one giant drawback: You need a bulky, ultraspecialized, kitchen-cluttering ice cream maker. How else are you going to incorporate air into the ice cream, reduce ice crystals, and lighten the texture for a smooth, silky final product? We wondered if we could tackle these goals using the multi-tasking food processor and a few clever ingredient tweaks instead. We started with a base of sweetened condensed milk and white chocolate. The sweetened condensed milk kept our ice cream velvety even after freezing, and the white chocolate gave it structure and silkiness. Both contributed rich flavor, as did heavy cream. A surprising ingredient—sour cream—added richness and tartness to counter the sweetness of the base. At first, we thought whipping the cream would be necessary to incorporate the air required for a smooth texture, but it turned out that simply mixing the unwhipped cream into the ice cream base gave us a much creamier, less icy end result, more like rich, dense premium ice cream (and it saved us a step). When it came to the freezing process, we knew that the quicker the base freezes, the smaller the ice crystals in the ice cream will be; and smaller ice crystals translate to smoother ice cream, so we sped things up by freezing the base in ice cube trays. Processing the frozen cubes incorporated enough air to turn them into a perfect vanilla ice cream. It took only a few quick alterations to make an equally pleasing chocolate version. Shop carefully: White chocolate varies greatly in quality. We like Guittard Choc-O-Lait Chips or Ghirardelli Classic White Chips. If you use a bar instead of chips, chop it fine before adding it to the processor. You will need 3 standard 16-cube ice cube trays for this recipe.

1 cup sweetened condensed milk	2½ cups heavy cream	⅛ teaspoon salt
⅓ cup (2 ounces) white chocolate chips	½ cup sour cream	
	2 tablespoons vanilla extract	

1 Microwave condensed milk in liquid measuring cup, stirring occasionally, until hot but not boiling, about 1 minute.

2 Add chocolate chips to food processor. With processor running, slowly add hot milk and process until chocolate is melted and smooth, about 1 minute, scraping down sides of bowl as needed. Add cream, sour cream, vanilla, and salt and process until well combined, about 30 seconds; transfer to 4-cup liquid measuring cup. Divide mixture evenly among 3 ice cube trays and freeze until solid, at least 24 hours.

3 Working in 4 batches, process frozen cubes in clean, dry processor until smooth and airy, about 30 seconds, scraping down sides of bowl as needed; transfer to airtight container and freeze while processing remaining cubes. Press plastic wrap directly on surface of ice cream and freeze until firm, at least 8 hours or up to 2 weeks. Serve.

EASIEST-EVER CHOCOLATE ICE CREAM

Omit sour cream and reduce vanilla to 1 teaspoon. Substitute 8 ounces bittersweet chocolate chips for white chocolate chips. Add 2 teaspoons instant espresso powder bloomed in 1 tablespoon hot water to processor with cream in step 2.

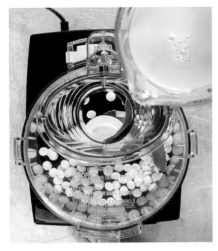

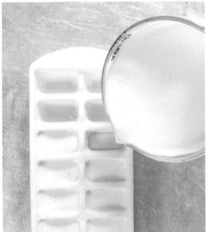

NO-FUSS BANANA ICE CREAM

makes about 1 quart   **food processor size** 7 to 14 cups

why this recipe works For a lighter alternative to classic ice cream that still had all the creaminess and flavor of the real thing, we turned to a pair of secret weapons: bananas and our food processor. Bananas were a perfect choice for our ice cream base: Their high pectin content allows them to remain creamy when frozen. We started by simply slicing whole, frozen, peeled bananas and then pureeing them in the food processor. Letting the bananas come to room temperature for 15 minutes before slicing made them easier to cut and kept the processing time to just 5 minutes. The end result had good banana flavor, but it wasn't quite as creamy as tasters wanted. We decided to try adding a little dairy to help achieve our desired consistency. We tested banana ice creams made with both milk and heavy cream; the version made with just ½ cup of heavy cream produced an unbeatable silky-smooth texture. Ripe, heavily speckled (or even black) bananas contained plenty of sweetness, so we skipped additional sugar. We did, however, add a bit of lemon juice, vanilla, and cinnamon to give our ice cream more dimension. Easy additions of cocoa powder or peanut butter gave us simple, flavorful variations. You can skip the freezing in step 2 and serve the ice cream immediately, but the texture will be softer.

6 very ripe bananas

½ cup heavy cream

1 tablespoon vanilla extract

1 teaspoon lemon juice

¼ teaspoon salt

¼ teaspoon ground cinnamon

1 Peel bananas, place in large zipper-lock bag, and press out excess air. Freeze bananas until solid, at least 8 hours.

2 Let bananas sit at room temperature to soften slightly, about 15 minutes. Slice into ½-inch-thick rounds and place in food processor. Add cream, vanilla, lemon juice, salt, and cinnamon and process until smooth, about 5 minutes, scraping down sides of bowl as needed. Transfer to airtight container, press plastic wrap directly on surface of ice cream, and freeze until firm, at least 2 hours or up to 5 days. Serve.

NO-FUSS PEANUT BUTTER–BANANA ICE CREAM
Reduce heavy cream to ¼ cup. Add ¼ cup peanut butter to processor with bananas.

NO-FUSS CHOCOLATE–BANANA ICE CREAM
Add ½ cup unsweetened cocoa powder to processor with bananas.

VANILLA MILKSHAKE

serves 2   food processor size 7 to 14 cups

why this recipe works For an old-fashioned soda fountain–style milkshake, we moved from the traditional blender to the food processor. The larger bowl of the food processor exposed more of the ice cream mixture to air and to the walls of the workbowl; this resulted in extra air being incorporated into the milkshakes, which made them lighter, frothier, and easier to sip through a straw. Also, the slightly higher heat generated by the food processor's blade caused more of the ice cream's tiny crystals to melt slightly, creating a smoother milkshake that remained cold but fluid. To amp up the vanilla flavor in our milkshake, we added a pinch of salt, which also offset the sweetness. Our simple ingredient list and food processor method made it easy to mix up different flavors. For a chocolate variation, we turned to cocoa powder (chocolate sauce was much too sweet), and we added malted milk powder for a complex, rounded flavor. Instant espresso powder created a coffee variation that wasn't too strong or bitter. Some extra salt and caramel sauce gave us a tasty salted caramel milkshake, and frozen strawberries, thawed and added to the processor, made for a vibrant strawberry shake. Serving these milkshakes in chilled glasses helps them stay colder longer. Our favorite vanilla ice cream is Ben & Jerry's Vanilla.

4 cups vanilla ice cream   ½ cup milk   Pinch salt

Let ice cream sit at room temperature to soften slightly, about 15 minutes. Process all ingredients in food processor until smooth, about 1 minute, scraping down sides of bowl as needed. Pour into chilled glasses and serve.

CHOCOLATE-MALT MILKSHAKE
Add ¼ cup malted milk powder and 1 tablespoon unsweetened cocoa powder to processor with other ingredients.

COFFEE MILKSHAKE
Add 2 teaspoons instant espresso powder to processor with other ingredients.

SALTED CARAMEL MILKSHAKE
Increase salt to ¼ teaspoon. Add ¼ cup caramel sauce to processor with other ingredients.

STRAWBERRY MILKSHAKE
Process 1 pound (3½ cups) thawed frozen strawberries in processor until smooth, about 1 minute, scraping down sides of bowl as needed. Reduce ice cream to 12 ounces (2 cups) and milk to ¼ cup and add to processor with pureed strawberries and salt.

CONVERSIONS AND EQUIVALENTS

Some say cooking is a science and an art. We would say that geography has a hand in it, too. Flours and sugars manufactured in the United Kingdom and elsewhere will feel and taste different from those manufactured in the United States. So we cannot promise that the loaf of bread you bake in Canada or England will taste the same as a loaf baked in the States, but we can offer guidelines for converting weights and measures. We also recommend that you rely on your instincts when making our recipes. Refer to the visual cues provided. If the dough hasn't "come together in a ball" as described, you may need to add more flour—even if the recipe doesn't tell you to. You be the judge.

The recipes in this book were developed using standard U.S. measures following U.S. government guidelines. The charts below offer equivalents for U.S. and metric measures. All conversions are approximate and have been rounded up or down to the nearest whole number.

Example

1 teaspoon = 4.9292 milliliters, rounded up to 5 milliliters
1 ounce = 28.3495 grams, rounded down to 28 grams

Volume Conversions

U.S.	METRIC
1 teaspoon	5 milliliters
2 teaspoons	10 milliliters
1 tablespoon	15 milliliters
2 tablespoons	30 milliliters
¼ cup	59 milliliters
⅓ cup	79 milliliters
½ cup	118 milliliters
¾ cup	177 milliliters
1 cup	237 milliliters
1¼ cups	296 milliliters
1½ cups	355 milliliters
2 cups (1 pint)	473 milliliters
2½ cups	591 milliliters
3 cups	710 milliliters
4 cups (1 quart)	0.946 liter
1.06 quarts	1 liter
4 quarts (1 gallon)	3.8 liters

Weight Conversions

OUNCES	GRAMS
½	14
¾	21
1	28
1½	43
2	57
2½	71
3	85
3½	99
4	113
4½	128
5	142
6	170
7	198
8	227
9	255
10	283
12	340
16 (1 pound)	454

Conversions for Common Baking Ingredients

Baking is an exacting science. Because measuring by weight is far more accurate than measuring by volume, and thus more likely to produce reliable results, in our recipes we provide ounce measures in addition to cup measures for many ingredients. Refer to the chart below to convert these measures into grams.

INGREDIENT	OUNCES	GRAMS
flour		
1 cup all-purpose flour*	5	142
1 cup cake flour	4	113
1 cup whole-wheat flour	5½	156
sugar		
1 cup granulated (white) sugar	7	198
1 cup packed brown sugar (light or dark)	7	198
1 cup confectioners' sugar	4	113
cocoa powder		
1 cup cocoa powder	3	85
butter†		
4 tablespoons (½ stick or ¼ cup)	2	57
8 tablespoons (1 stick or ½ cup)	4	113
16 tablespoons (2 sticks or 1 cup)	8	227

* U.S. all-purpose flour, the most frequently used flour in this book, does not contain leaveners, as some European flours do. These leavened flours are called self-rising or self-raising. If you are using self-rising flour, take this into consideration before adding leaveners to a recipe.

† In the United States, butter is sold both salted and unsalted. We generally recommend unsalted butter. If you are using salted butter, take this into consideration before adding salt to a recipe.

Oven Temperatures

FAHRENHEIT	CELSIUS	GAS MARK
225	105	¼
250	120	½
275	135	1
300	150	2
325	165	3
350	180	4
375	190	5
400	200	6
425	220	7
450	230	8
475	245	9

Converting Temperatures from an Instant-Read Thermometer

We include doneness temperatures in many of the recipes in this book. We recommend an instant-read thermometer for the job. Refer to the table above to convert Fahrenheit degrees to Celsius. Or, for temperatures not represented in the chart, use this simple formula:

Subtract 32 degrees from the Fahrenheit reading, then divide the result by 1.8 to find the Celsius reading.

Example:
"Roast chicken until thighs register 175 degrees."
To convert:

$$175°F - 32 = 143°$$
$$143° \div 1.8 = 79.44°C, \text{ rounded down to } 79°C$$

Index